Written on the Heart
And Other Sermon that Matters

Forrest Krummel

Parson's Porch Books
www.parsonsporchbooks.com

Written on the Heart and Other Sermons that Matter
ISBN: Softcover 978-1-949888-75-1
Copyright © 2019 by Forrest Krummel

All rights reserved. No part of this book may be reproduced or transmitted in any form or by any means, electronic or mechanical, including photocopying, recording, or by any information storage and retrieval system, without permission in writing from the publisher.

Written on the Heart

Contents

Introduction 9

The Ring 11
    Luke 15: 1-3, 11b-32; II Corinthians 5: 16-21

Second Chances and Missed Opportunities 16
    Luke 13: 1-9; Isaiah 55: 1-9

What Is Your Jerusalem? 20
    Genesis 15: 1-12, 17-18; Luke 13: 31-35

Rock Tumbler: The Temptations of Jesus 24
    Luke 4: 1-13

A Glimpse of Grace at a Fish Fry 27
    II Corinthians 5:20b-6:10

God Is Greater Than Our Prejudices 29
    Luke 4: 21-30

The Fourth Gift 34
    Matthew 2: 1-12

Who Do You Think You Are? 40
    Ephesians 1: 3-14

Fools for Christ 46
    Mark 16: 1-8; John 20: 1-10; Luke 24: 1-12

A Way Out of No Way 49
    Genesis 17: 1-16

True Religion 54
    James 1: 17-27; Mark 7: 1-8, 15-15, 21-23

Sugar for the Soul 59
    Luke 6: 17-26, Jeremiah 17: 56-10, Psalm 1 59

Relationship Over Revenge 63
   Genesis 45: 3-11, 15; Psalm 37: 1-7; I Corinthians 15: 35-38, 42-50; Luke 6: 27-38

The God Who Embraced Me 70
   Psalm 147: 1-11, 20c

Simple Math 74
   James 3: 13-4:3, 7-8

Wind and Fire 77
   Joel 2:28

A Promise is a Promise: God Keeps Promises 81
   Genesis 9: 8-17 81

Roots and Wings 85
   John 17:1-15

Written on the Heart 90
   Jeremiah 31: 31-34; John 12: 20-33

How Much Does It Cost? 92
   II Corinthians 8: 7-15

The Power of Words 96
   James 1: 17-27

Can Faith Save You? 101
   James 2: 1-17

Tongues of Fire 105
   James 3: 1-12

Grace Along the Appalachian Trail 110
   John 10: 11-18

God in the Silence 116
   Luke 2: 41-52

Under Armour 121
  Ephesians 6
Be Careful How You Live 125
  Ephesians 5: 15-20
It's Not About You 129
  Ephesians 2: 1-10

Introduction

Parson's Porch Books is delighted to present to you this series called Sermons Matter.

We believe that many of the best writers are pastors who take the role of preacher seriously. Week in, and week out, they exegete scripture, research material, write and deliver sermons in the context of the life of their particular congregation in their given community.

We further believe that sermons are extensions of Holy Scripture which need to be published beyond the manuscripts which are written for delivery each Sunday. Books serve as a vehicle for the sermon to continue to proclaim the Good News of the Morning to a broader audience.

We celebrate the wonderful occasion of the preaching event in Christian worship when the Pastor speaks, the People listen and the Work of the Church proceeds.

Take, Read, and Heed.

David Russell Tullock, M.Div., D.Min.

Publisher
Parson's Porch Books

The Ring

Luke 15: 1-3, 11b-32; II Corinthians 5: 16-21

But the father said to his servants, "Bring quickly the best robe, and put it on him; and put a ring on his hand... (v. 22)

Humorist Garrison Keillor once said that "The Gospel is meant to comfort the afflicted and afflict the comfortable."

This gospel lesson is one of, if not the most familiar of Jesus' parables. Almost everyone can identify with it--a father or mother who patiently waits for their son or daughter to "return to their senses", the individual who squandered opportunities, the person who wonders about "fairness".

Noted author, preacher, and scholar Barbara Brown Taylor observed that "the problem with a really good parable--especially one as beloved as this one--is that it can become "limp" from use. It becomes a kind of Velveteen Rabbit easily draped over a shoulder or cast aside. I call this "taming" the gospel so that it neither harms nor challenges.

But, the gospel of Jesus Christ is not tame. We've been walking through Luke's story of Jesus and from the very beginning we have been told that Jesus turns the world upside down. The gospel is about a reversal of fortunes; the haves become have nots and the have nots become haves. Those clothed in the purple splendor of this world will find themselves in a place of torment in the Next while the forgotten and neglected Lazaruses of this world find themselves nestled in the loving bosom of Father Abraham in the Next.

The late Fred Craddock said that this parable (the Prodigal Son) has been embraced by many people "who have not felt the full impact of the offense of grace that it dramatically conveys." I will repeat that because I want you to wrap your head around what I just said. This parable has been embraced by people "who have not felt the full impact of the offense of grace it dramatically conveys.

The parable of the Prodigal is the third of three parables that Jesus used when he responded to the criticism of the Pharisees and keepers of the Law when they questioned the nature of his ministry and the company he kept. He welcomed tax collectors and sinners, the riff-raff and unclean, the misfits and nobodies.

The first parable was of a man who had 100 sheep. One of them wandered off so he left the 99 to go find it. This is simply not good husbandry. It is foolish because by the time the shepherd found the one lost sheep the other 99 could have scattered in 99 different directions as they grazed. Yet, Jesus said, there is more joy in heaven over one sinner who repents than over 99 righteous person who need no repentance. (vss. 4-9)

The second parable was about a lost coin. A woman searched high and low for one lost coin and called in her friends and neighbors to celebrate when it is found. "Just so, I tell you," Jesus said, "there is joy before the angels of God over one sinner who repents." (vss. 8-10)

So far, Jesus had not moved into the "discomfort zone". He crossed into that territory with the parable of "The Prodigal." Now a "prodigal" is someone who is "recklessly extravagant." In his book, *The Prodigal God: Recovering the Heart of the Christian Faith*, Timothy Keller believes that it is the father who is the true prodigal. He is the one who is reckless in giving his youngest son his inheritance. And he is the one who is reckless in begging his eldest son to rejoice in the return of his younger brother. The only thing important to the father is "relationship"; relationship with each of his sons and his sons with each other. Whether this is a reconciliation between the brothers we don't know, nor will we ever know. Jesus left the parable open ended. Maybe he did this because it is up to us to right the story. After all, our epistle lesson this morning told us that God "reconciled us to himself through Christ and has given to us the ministry of reconciliation. So we are ambassadors for Christ, since God is making his appeal through us. (vss. 19-20)

The eldest son was concerned with justice and fairness. In his youngest brother he saw someone who squandered a seemingly once in a lifetime opportunity. He wanted his brother to suffer the consequences, after all, he made his bed; now he should sleep in it. But instead, he is received by the father as if nothing ever happened, all was forgiven, all was forgotten. Where is the justice in that? Where is the fairness?

I had a conversation not too long ago with a child about fairness. It was unfair that because a few students acted up that the whole class was punished. it is unfair in the military that just because one member of a unit messes up that the whole unit is disciplined. It is unfair that because one player on a team doesn't perform that the whole team has to run laps. I told the child that life is full of things that are "unfair" but when we spend our time looking for "fairness" we are walking on the thin ice of victimhood. We need to play the cards that we are dealt not wish for a different or better hand.

A few days ago I walked back from a church tutoring program. I was taken aside and told of some family situations that are not fair to the children; neglect, troubled parents and siblings, abuse, getting caught in the net of the social services "system". And I thought to myself, where is the fairness in any of these children's homelife. Or for that matter, where is the fairness that I was born in the United States to loving parents who sacrificed much so that I could be better off than they were while another child is born into a different family or even a different country; into a home in a neighborhood where children cannot go outside to play because of gunfire or into a home where food is used as a weapon and famine is rampant?

But here is the real scandal of this lesson. It is the ring. Scholars debate what kind of ring it was. Based on the other parables that preceded this parable AND based on the context that it is in response to the criticism of the Pharisees and keepers of the Law, I suspect that the ring was the father's signet ring. In other words, total restoration. There is no reason to think that when the father died that the younger son would not get his portion of the inheritance as if nothing had ever happened. As God said through the prophet Isaiah, "I am He who blots out your transgressions for my own sake, and I will not remember your sins. (43:25)

No wonder the elder son was upset. It wasn't fair. This is the offense of grace; it isn't fair. But then, if it was fair, it wouldn't be grace, would it?!

Now, here's the question: Are you okay with this offensive grace? If you're not then older brother and you have a lot in common. It's something to think about. Amen.

Second Chances and Missed Opportunities

Luke 13: 1-9; Isaiah 55: 1-9

March 24, 1980 was a bright and sunny morning in San Salvador, El Salvador. Outside the Church of the Divine Providence a car stopped. A lone gunman stepped out and rested his rifle on the car door. Peering through the scope, past the open door of the church and down the long center aisle he focused on Oscar Romero, the Roman Catholic archbishop of El Salvador. Father Romero was in middle of saying mass. As Romero held up the "host" the gunman pulled the trigger. A crack echoed off of the buildings. A red disk appeared on the front of the archbishop's white vestments. Romero staggered a couple of steps before falling. A pool of blood soaked the little white disks of the now scattered host. Oscar Romero's assassin was never captured.

This past March 3 dark storm clouds gathered over Lee County, Alabama. No one could guess what would soon follow. A black swirling funnel suddenly dropped from the clouds, a tornado with winds up to 170 miles an hour and four times as wide as the typical tornado tore through farms and homes. Within a matter of minutes 23 people died as the tornado a path a mile wide.

Nearly two weeks ago on March 15 a 28-year-old Australian and self-proclaimed white supremist parked outside two mosques in Christchurch, New Zealand. He used five semi-automatic weapons as he fired upon worshipers going to prayer--men, women, and children. Before he was through 49 worshipers lay dead. A 50th died a few days later.

In our gospel lesson Luke tells us of a time when Pilate ordered a "hit" on Galileans as they worshiped. Like Romero's blood soaking the host, their blood mingled with the blood of their sacrifices.

"Do you think", Jesus asked upon hearing the story, "that because these Galileans suffered in this way (that) they were worse sinners than other Galileans? No. But unless you repent, you will all perish as they did.

Then Jesus continued. "Or what about those eighteen who were killed when the tower of Siloam (in Jerusalem) fell upon them? Do you think that they were offenders than all the others living in Jerusalem? No, I tell you; but unless you repent, you will all perish as they did. (vss. 2-5)

A call to repentance in the face of such horrific events seems so out of place, doesn't it? Why would Jesus say such a thing? It's certainly not something that we would say, is it? What was Jesus really saying?

Jesus didn't say that the people killed at the altar or by the fall of the tower of Siloam did anything wrong. They didn't deserve what happened to them. They were simply minding their own business, going about their lives when their lives ended abruptly.

The Psalmist asked God to "teach us to number our days that we may gain a heart of wisdom." (90:12)

Life is short and uncertain. Time, our time is not limitless. "Seek the Lord while he may be found" our Old Testament lesson says, "...let the wicked forsake their way, and the unrighteous their thoughts." (Isaiah 55: 6 & 7)

Ordinarily we think of "repentance" as "turning around" or to stop doing something wrong. But that is just one understanding of repentance. Repentance also means "to gain a new point of view", to get a new perspective, to see the world as God sees the world.

It is only when we understand this that Jesus' parable of the fig tree makes sense. The fig tree was planted three years before the owner of the vineyard looked for fruit only to find none. Fig trees bear fruit after two years. It is completely understandable for the owner of the vineyard to tell his gardener to cut the tree down to make room for another tree because this tree was obviously wasting good soil. It was unfruitful. It had its chance and didn't produce.

The gardener, though, asked for more time. "Give it one more year--one more chance. I will dig around it and put manure on it. If after this second chance it does bear fruit, great. But if it doesn't, then I will cut it down."

I do not know if you've been watching the NCAA tournament or not. You may be keeping a bracket. You've seen upsets and comebacks. You've felt disappointment. But as you know, each game has a limited amount to time before it is over. James Howell noted that God's greatest gift to each one of us is "time". Each one of us has a limited amount of time before the game of our life comes to an end. We have a limited amount to time to do the work that God placed us on this earth to do. There is time for second chances, sure, and even comebacks, but we do not have forever.

You see, this lesson is not about the way we die. It is about the way we live.

To God be the glory. Amen.

What Is Your Jerusalem?
Genesis 15: 1-12, 17-18; Luke 13: 31-35

At that very hour some Pharisees came and said to him, "Get away from here, for Herod wants to kill you." (Luke 13: 31)

Today's gospel lesson is puzzling; Pharisees coming to Jesus and warning him not to go to Jerusalem because Herod wants to kill him? Why the warning? Could it be that some of Jesus' followers were Pharisees? Maybe. Could it be that Jesus himself was a Pharisee? Possibly. As we learned in the Monday bible studies, we don't really know much about the historical Jesus. We know the Christ of faith.

It could also be, though, that the Pharisees that came warning Jesus didn't want him to go to Jerusalem because of the ruckus that he would cause, thus threatening their standing. Afterall, when he did go into Jerusalem, Luke tells us that he went in with a parade and that he took a whip as he turned over the tables of the money-changers in the Temple.

This possibility got me to thinking, "What is our Jerusalem?" Where would we prefer Jesus not to go in our lives. We are sorely tempted to be inoculated with Jesus--only getting enough of Jesus to making us immune to catching a full-blown case of taking Jesus seriously. We wish to take him seriously when it suits us but not so seriously as to inconvenience us.

This past week as the music director, Russel and I met with Dr. Cory Ganschow, the visiting choral director, prepared for this morning, we talked about how we can arrange the chancel area to seat their chorale. In the course of the discussion Russell noted that I always like to have the baptismal font front and center, especially when it is inconvenient because I believe that our baptism should inconvenience us. Our baptism reminds us that we are on the road to taking Jesus seriously. The decisions we make, the values that we hold, and the actions we take should be affected by our commitment to taking Jesus seriously. "Show me your works, and I will show you your faith" the Letter of James reminds us. What you believe is betrayed by your actions.

The late Robert Munger delivered a sermon while he was at the University Presbyterian Church in Berkley, California entitled, "My Heart, Christ's Home". In it he used the metaphor of Christ taking up residence in our heart. A little house cleaning is in order. There is the study, the place where we train the mind, the dining room where we feed our body and spirit, the living room where we spend our leisure hours, the rec room where we gather with the company we keep and entertain--cut loose.

But there is also one more room, or rather the hall closet, to be exact. An odor emanates from it like there is something dead inside. This is our Jerusalem. The place that we declare off-limits, out-of-bounds to Christ. Jesus is welcomed everywhere but here.

For some of us it is the way we spend our money. Money is neither innately good nor bad. It just "is". It builds hospitals to the benefit of a community or it can buy admission to major universities to the detriment of meritocracy. In the synoptic gospels of Matthew, Mark, and Luke Jesus the real turning point is when Jesus turned over the tables of the money-changers in the Temple. He hit them in the pocketbook and thus crossed the line between "preaching and meddling." Our values are most clearly revealed in the way we spend our money, individually, as a corporation, a nonprofit, or a congregation.

"Where your treasure is, there will be your heart also," Jesus told his listeners in the Sermon on the Mount. The opposite is also true; where your heart is, there will also be your treasure. Follow the money, investigators say. "It's all about the money", Troy Ave(nue) rapped.

For others of us Jerusalem is our home. I will never forget the conversation that I had with a wife and daughter of a man as we talked about his funeral. When I asked about their best memory of this man I was met with a curious silence. Finally the wife broke the silence saying, "I know that you have to say nice things about my husband because he was a well-respected professional as well as a church and civic leader. But that is not who he was at home.

For still others, Jerusalem is the business world. We do not want Jesus to see the business decisions that we make, the corners that we cut, the rules that we bend or break.

All of us have a Jerusalem, that place where we do not want Jesus to go; that place where we like to think that God does not see or know about. But here's the thing; Jesus goes to Jerusalem. God knows that which we try so desperately to hide. All of this may seem like bad news, but it is also good news, gospel. Jesus went to Jerusalem where he was celebrated one day, betrayed, denied, and crucified before the week's end. But the story did not end there. We are journeying toward Easter where the best news is found. The news that the women first heard so long ago that still gives hope today.

Jesus also travels to our own individual Jerusalems, the Jerusalem of our individual hearts. He cannot be deterred. He will not be denied. His love is too great.

Amen.

Rock Tumbler: The Temptations of Jesus

Luke 4: 1-13

> *Jesus, full of the Holy Spirit, returned from the Jordan and was led by the Spirit in the wilderness, 2 where for forty days he was tempted by the devil.* (Luke 4: 1-2a)

My father-in-law was a man who had to always be busy. As a consequence he was also a man of many hobbies; vegetable gardening, roses, latch-hook rugs, and rock polishing. When he died, I was "bequeathed" his rock polisher. It was a rubber canister about six inches in diameter that set upon a motorized base that would spin it over and over and over.

Rock polishing takes a lot of time and patience. You take a handful of stones to be polished, drop them in the canister, add some water and grit, seal, and set it on the base. Then you wait as the canister spins day after day after day. After several week, you remove the stones from the canister, add water and a finer grit, and repeat the process. You did this over and over until after a few months the stones are removed a final time, rinsed off, and reveal their shiny beauty, a beauty that had been hidden. It is the grit and the rubbing against one another that reveals their true character. So it is with temptation. Over the course of a lifetime, temptation reveals are true character.

What is your greatest temptation? My wife once observed in a sermon that we are not tempted by that which we don't desire or want. For example, if you don't like chocolate, you will not be tempted by either a fresh batch of chocolate chip cookies or Ghirardelli chocolate squares.

In the first book of the Bible, Genesis, we read that the first of our kind were tempted by "the fruit of the tree that produced fruit that was good to eat, pleasing to the eye, and desirable for gaining wisdom." (3:6)

Temptation comes in all different forms, shapes, and sizes. Some people are tempted by money or titles, others by control or power, still others by fame or recognition.

The story of Jesus' temptation is familiar to many, if not all of us. It occurred immediately after his baptism. And to me, the most interesting thing about his temptations is not what he was tempted with but the fact that he was led into the wilderness of temptation by the Spirit of God. His temptations were not accidental but intentional.

The story about Jesus' temptations per se but the choices Jesus made. Seek first the Kingdom of God and God's righteousness and all these things shall be added unto you, Jesus told those who would take him seriously. In his response to temptation Jesus placed his ultimate trust in God. In these 40 days of Lent we are to choose where we will ultimately place our trust.

"In life and death we belong to God", or as the Letter to the Romans states it, if we live, we live unto the Lord and if we die, we die unto the Lord, so whether we live or whether we die, we belong to the Lord. (14:8)

In her commentary on this passage Lori Brandt Hale wrote that "there is a spiritual depth and power for life that is made possible as we respond in faith to the trials, troubles, and temptations of life". Life's temptations are the grit that reveals who we really are. The Table to which we are invited reminds us that as God provided manna to Israel in the Old Testament wilderness of the Sinai, so God's angels ministered to Jesus. God still ministers to us by providing our daily bread for Life's Journey.

In this season of Lent we have a choice to make. Which do we trust more, God's Providential care or the world? To God be the glory, Amen.

A Glimpse of Grace at a Fish Fry
II Corinthians 5:20b-6:10

A few weeks ago I attended a neighborhood fish fry. Now one of the things that you need to know about my neighborhood is that the overwhelming majority of people that go to church are Roman Catholic since "St. Phil's" is within walking distance. Early in the evening I noticed that one of my neighbors was holding a glass of red wine. Now, I have never seen this neighbor hold anything other than a bottle of beer--not a can, but a bottle. I jokingly said something to him and as he looked at his glass his wife volunteered, "Oh, he loves red wine. Besides, he's giving up beer for Lent!" Everyone, including myself, laughed.

Later, though, I got to thinking; it seems that whenever someone talks about giving something up for Lent, they usually give up something that is not "healthy" for them--beer, wine, dessert, chocolate, and the like, only to resume them after Easter. Where's the penance in that?!

If we insist on giving something up why don't we give up things that are hurtful and mean; gossip, slander, hostility, prejudice, vengeance, for example. Or, better yet, instead of giving something up, why don't we begin something new? Generosity, praise, forgiveness, tolerance; things like that.

On Ash Wednesday we are asked to remember that we are passing shadows on the face of this planet. We came from dust and to dust we shall return. We are encouraged to take a moral and spiritual inventory in the hope of discovering or recovering the purpose that God gave and gives to us. The communion table around which we will gather reminds us that God is with us on our journey, encouraging us to become better selves.

In this Lent may we dedicate ourselves to glorifying God through our words and actions as we attempt to make this a truly holy Lent.

God Is Greater Than Our Prejudices

Luke 4: 21-30

> *"Yet Elijah was sent to none of them except to a widow of Zarephath in Sidon." (v. 26)*

All of us have prejudices. Now we do not like to admit it, but we do. Prejudices are preconceived notions that are based on limited facts at best. It is "knowing" what you do not know. Years ago Sue and I experienced this first hand. Serving as youth ministers the music department had a preconceived notion of who we were, based not on their experience with us, but upon their experience with our predecessors. They could not see us as being just like them.

Prejudice is also based on the hue of our skin, our zip code, the schools we attend, and so forth. None of us are without prejudice. The problem with prejudice is not only that it is shallow but that it is misleading. A bigger problem is when we place upon God our own prejudices and bias.

Someone once said, "God made humanity in the divine image, and humanity returned the favor!"

That quip came to my mind as I reflected upon today's gospel. Picture the scene. Jesus returned to his hometown, Nazareth. As a "guest preacher" he was handed the scroll of the prophet Isaiah. He read the assigned text for the day, Isaiah 61: 1 and 2.

The Spirit of the Lord is upon me,

because he has anointed me
to bring good news to the poor.
He has sent me to proclaim release to the captives
and recovery of sight to the blind
to let the oppressed go free,
to proclaim the year of the Lord's favor."

Closing the scroll "all spoke well of (Jesus)" and were amazed at his "gracious words." No doubt, some remembered him as Joseph and Mary's little boy, the one that they brought to the Temple; the one who was always asking questions. Now, they simply marveled. They may have even poked one another and nodded their approval.

But Jesus did not seek their accolades or approval. He wanted to drive home a point. He was never one to leave well enough alone. Realizing that they did not fully comprehend the significance of his words--" today this reading has been fulfilled in your hearing", Jesus reminded the congregation of who God is. Did they remember two of their own prophets, Elijah and Elisha.

In a time of a drought and famine, at a time when there were many widows in Israel--people who had no one care provide for them--God sent Elijah not to one of Israel's houses but to the house of the widow of Zarephath, a foreigner. It was in her house that he performed a miracle feeding. Now, this got the congregation's attention.

Jesus continued. At a time when there were many lepers in Israel, Elisha cleansed a foreigner, a Syrian general named Naaman. At this thing turned ugly. The congregation grew angry and wanted to kill this self-proclaimed prophet, this hometown boy, this son of Joseph, this Jesus. Just who did he think he was to push their narrow boundaries of God. "Blessed assurance, God is min, not yours!"

God does not share our prejudices. In the story of Jonah (which I am teaching in our midweek Logos program, we read that when Jonah went off on a pout God reminded him the Divine's compassion and care not just for those whom Jonah loved or liked, but for all of God's Creation, all of God's children. God was and is concerned with the plight of the foreigner, the alien, the lost, the last, and the lonely, even if they were not. This is a very hard pill to swallow. What God may see things differently than we do?! Impossible, isn't it?

Jesus was not setting down something new and unheard of. He reminds us God's command.

Exodus 22:21 "Do not mistreat an alien or oppress him, for you were aliens in Egypt.

Exodus 23:9 "You shall not oppress an alien, … for you were aliens in the land of Egypt.

Leviticus 19:33-34 "'When an alien lives with you in your land, do not mistreat him. The stranger who lives as a foreigner with you shall be to you as the native-born among you, and you shall love him as yourself; for you lived as foreigners in the land of Egypt. I am Yahweh your God.

Deuteronomy 24: 17-18 Do not deprive the alien or the fatherless of justice or take the cloak of the widow as a pledge. Remember that you were slaves in Egypt and the LORD your God redeemed you from there. That is why I command you to do this.

Jesus reminded them that they were the "Chosen People" to care for all of God's Creation. They were chosen for service not safety. And we, who take Jesus seriously, are "saved to serve". With "privilege" comes "responsibility". "God made humanity in the divine image and humanity returned the favor."

God is not limited by our prejudices. God is a big god, not a small one limited by our likes and dislikes, preconceived notions and prejudices. Jesus, we are told, simply "passed through the crowd and went on his way." (v.30) I believe that the Risen Lord still does that. Those who are blinded or constrained by their prejudices are simply "passed through" as the Risen Lord goes on his way--the way to Truth and Life.

When we pray "Thy will be done, on earth as it is in heaven" we are not giving God permission because God n-e-v-e-r needs permission. Instead we are acknowledging that God's will be done on earth and we can either get on board or get run over.

The sacrament that we are about to celebrate is about a Love greater than our prejudice. This is God's act of Grace, not ours. The Table is not our table but God's. It is God who issues the invitation through the clay vessel of human voice and speech. It is not a Table for the worthy but for those who recognize their unworthiness. It is open to all, not the few. At the Table we touch and taste Good News. Amen.

The Fourth Gift
Matthew 2: 1-12

"We have observed his star at its rising and have come to pay homage." (v. 2)

How many of you made "New Year's Resolutions?" How many of you have already broken a resolution or two? There is an old Yiddish saying that is appropriate for our resolutions. "Mann tracht, un Gott lacht"; which translates into: "We plan, and God laughs." One of my favorite New Year's Resolutions is, "Resolved: Do better and love Jesus!"

*****

Over the next few weeks we reflect upon New Year's Resolutions. We will look at how to "love Jesus and do better," but, if we listen carefully enough to the silence of our soul, we may even hear God laugh.

*****

Modern American Christian culture has woven the story of Epiphany into the Christmas narrative. Tradition says that there were three wise men bearing gifts--gold, frankincense, and myrrh. Witty women are fond of pointing out if the wise men had been women they would have arrived on time, helped deliver the baby, brought practical gifts, cleaned the stable, made a casserole, and that there would be peace on earth!

Humor aside, the story does not say how many "wise men" there were, just that there were three gifts. Nor does it say that they are kings. They were "magi" which means that they would have been astrologers, members of the Persian priestly caste, or possibly Zoroastrians from Persia or Babylon which today would be Iraq or Iran.

In telling his story Matthew carefully wove together pagan astrology and Jewish prophetic voice; a star heralding the cosmic event and a shepherd kind from Bethlehem in the land of Judah. Matthew's intention is clear; in the birth of This Child God was doing something new that would change the world, the whole world. In the words of the apostle, "The old has passed away; the new has come." (II Corinthians 5:17) The world would undergo a "rebirth". The apostle Paul wrote about this in his Letter to the Romans:

I consider that the suffering of this present time is not worth with the glory that is to be revealed to us. ... We know that they whole world has been groaning in travail (as in childbirth) until now. (8: 18 & 22)

The birth of this new world order would be painful, but the joy that it will bring far outweighs the pain of the moment.

It is the "birth" of this "new world order" that terrified Herod the Great "and all of Jerusalem".

The "new", the "different", and "change" itself is always hard. It is always met with conscious or unconscious, intentional or unintentional sabotage and resistance. Tell someone that you want to lose 20 pounds that they will offer you a cookie, saying: "What's one cookie? Surely that won't matter. Besides, I just made them for you!" It is this resistance to change that causes so many of our New Year's Resolutions to fail.

And, it was resistance to change that motivated Herod to inquire of chief priests and scribes of Jerusalem where the Messiah was to be born. It was why he asked the visitors from the East to be sure to tell him where he might find the Child they sought. And it ultimately caused what theologians call "the slaughter of the innocent" later in Matthew's gospel.

*****

The gifts the Magi brought are interesting not just for what they were but for what was added. In our Call to Worship from the prophet of Isaiah the visitors from the East brought two gifts: gold and frankincense. But Matthew records a third gift, "myrrh".

Gold has always been viewed as a gift "fit for a king", but frankincense and myrrh? Well, that deserves more exploration. Both are fragrant substances acquired from distant exotic lands at great expense. They were also royal favorites.

Frankincense was the "holy perfume" used exclusively in the sanctuary. Was the place where Jesus lay the "sanctuary" of this new reign, this new world order, this new Kingdom? Was Matthew pointing to the day when the risen and glorified "Messiah" would be worshiped as God "the Father"?

Myrrh is an interesting addition to the Isaiah words. It was used as an anointing oil by the High Priest. Was this Matthew's subtle way of reminding or telling his community that Jesus is "the Anointed One" or the Christ at his birth?

In John's gospel we are told that Nicodemus brought a hundred pound mixture of aloe and myrrh to prepare the body of Jesus for burial. Was the addition of myrrh Matthew's way of pointing to the Crucifixion and what lay beyond?

*****

These are the three gifts of the Magi but there was also a Fourth Gift. It is mentioned three times in the gospel lesson. This Fourth Gift is homage. Another word for homage is worship.

*****

"We have observed the star and come to pay him homage", the Magi told Herod.

"Go and search diligently for the child," Herod told the Magi, "that I may also go and pay him homage."

"Upon entering the house, (the Magi) saw the child with his mother Mary; and they knelt down and paid him homage."

*****

In feudal times to "pay homage" was to make oneself a vessel-- an instrument--to a lord. It was to bow down and humble oneself. The earliest confession in the Church was a simple three-word statement: "Jesus is Lord." "If we live, we live unto the Lord," Paul wrote, "and if we die, we die unto the Lord; so in both life and death we belong to the Lord." (Romans 14:8)

In a few minutes we will set aside men and women to take on positions of responsibility in this congregation and in Christ's greater Church. They will be asked if they trust in Jesus Christ as Savior, acknowledge Him as Lord of all and the head of the Church. This church does not belong to us--it does not belong to any one generation.

I remember years ago a child was walking home from a school that sat across the street from the church that I served at the time. Seeing me come out of the building he asked me if I owned the church. I told him that I did not. He then asked who owned the church. I paused for a moment as I considered his question and then answered honestly, "God does." Satisfied he walked on home.

God owns the small "c" and big "C" church. We are mere stewards, temporary tenants. Nothing more. We do the best we can, living together and always striving to balance the "peace, unity, and purity" of the church. How we do this is another sermon for another day. But for now, suffice it to say our first New Year's Resolution will be to be like the Magi who sought the Christ Child to pay homage. May we strive to humble ourselves and acknowledge that Christ is Lord of all--our possessions, our treasure, and our very lives. May we not go a single day without asking God what we should do, that the Divine guide us in our thoughts and actions. And may we remember that we are nothing more than humble servants in the service of the King of kings.

To God be the glory. Amen.

Who Do You Think You Are?
Ephesians 1: 3-14

> *Blessed be the God and Father of our Lord Jesus Christ, who has blessed us in Christ with every spiritual blessing in the heavenly places, just as God chose us in Christ before the foundation of the world to be holy and blameless before God in love.* (vss. 3 & 4)

Who Do You Think You Are is one of those British imports that American audiences fall in love with. It's not a Downton Abbey-like import, but an America's Got Talent-like import. Each week a well-known personality is taken on a genealogical quest of who they are. In America the subjects have included football play Emmitt Smith, film producer Spike Lee, actors Jon Cryer of "Two and a Half Men", Hilary Duff, and Brooke Shields, to name only a few. Sometimes family lore is debunked, secrets revealed, suspicions confirmed as well as tears, laughter, pride and a better understanding of who they really are.

We are a genetic composite of our ancestors who preceded us. Have you ever said something to your children and then thought to yourself, "Oooh, that sounds just like my dad" or "my mother"? Have you ever looked in the mirror and seen the shadow of your mother or father staring back at you? Have you looked at old family pictures and have someone say that you look just like a grandfather or grandmother, an aunt or an uncle?

Counselors trained in "family systems" will tell you that certain behavioral patterns replicate themselves in subsequent generations; alcoholism, divorce, or a propensity to a certain illness. Someone I know decided to go to counseling because they wanted to work on their marriage end "the pattern of divorce" while their children were still young. They wanted to set a new example and establish a "new normal".

One of the woes that academics have is the increasing number of Americans who simply don't know and don't care about our own country's history. British orator, philosopher and legislator Edmund Burke once said that those who do not know history are doomed to repeat it.

It can be difficult and painful to come face to face with our history, our family tree. We may see a rotten apple or two and even be surprised at seeing an apricot on the ol' family apple tree. And, it is easy to forget "whose" we are, especially when we don't know who we are. Jesus once told a parable about this. It is commonly called the parable of the prodigal son but, as Timothy Keller wrote in his book by the same name, it's really about a "prodigal father" who was extravagant in his grace.

Over the next few weeks we are going to systematically walk through the New Testament letter to the Ephesians. We will begin by exploring the question, "Who do you think you are?"

Because of a variety of internal factors, most biblical scholars believe that this letter was written after the death of the apostle Paul by one of Paul's premier students. The writer encapsulated the great apostle's teaching in what would become a circular letter.

The letter begins with the customary salutation before reminding us who we are. We are Chosen, Holy and Blameless. I invited you to look at those three words with me.

Chosen. You are not an accident. We are not an accident. This congregation is not an accident. We are Chosen; we are chosen before the foundation of the world. In the words of the old hymn,

I sought the Lord, and afterward I knew,
he moved my soul to seek him seeking me;
it was not I that found O Savior true,
no, I was found of thee.

In his farewell discourse found in the gospel of John Jesus told his disciples, you did not choose me, but I chose you. And I appointed you to go and bear fruit. (16:15) Jesus calls us in the tumult of life's wild seas not for positions of privilege but for service in God's Eternal Kingdom. God has work for us to do. And God has given us the equipment for our work of repairers of the breach and setting right the brokenness of the world. To do this, we have been infused with holiness.

Holiness. In the First Letter of Peter the writer said that the Christian community and individuals of that community are to (and I quote): "prepare your minds for action; discipline yourselves … like obedient children do not be conformed to the desires that you formerly had. … Instead, as the One who called you is holy, be holy yourselves in all your conduct, as it is written, "You shall be holy, for I am holy. (1: 13-16, selected)

To be holy is to be different. The Early Church, the first century Church never doubted that it had to be different from the culture in which it found itself. That is why they were persecuted.

Danish philosopher once Soren Kierkegaard once shared a parable called "Tame Geese". In this parable he describes a barnyard where a flock of geese lived. Each Sunday they would waddle out of their houses and waddle down the main street to their church. They would waddle to their pew in a grand cathedral. There would be a geese choir that would sing beautifully before a goose pastor would read from the geese bible. The goose minister would do some version of the same message every week.

"My fellow geese, God has given you wings! With these wings you can fly! With these wings you can soar like eagles! No walls can confine you; no fences can hold you. You have wings and you can fly like the birds God created you to be!"

The geese would nod and quack--do geese quack? --their approval before waddling home. Some became Christmas dinner. Some were sold. But none ever flew.

The biggest criticism of the modern Church is that for too long it has been indistinguishable from the world in which it exists. The Church has essentially said that we will not expect too much from you. We will not challenge you too much or make you too uncomfortable. All you have to do in exchange is to live a relatively good, decent and respectable life.

As a consequence the Church has become socially acceptable-- or at least tolerated-- Europe and North America. But, over time, as too many churches became a nice place to go, on a nice Sunday morning, where a person could sit in a nice comfortable worship space, hear a nice talk before going to a nice lunch, and return to a nice home, to send children to nice schools and go to a nice job, the church has become more and more politicized and increasingly irrelevant. You see, the problem with nice is that it is boring and easily manipulated.

Jesus Christ did not call his disciples out of the world but into the world. He called those who would take him seriously to make a difference within the world. Christ didn't call for "Christian" doctors, nurses, lawyers, counselors, business leaders, workers, homemakers, child care workers, employers, or whatever. Rather he called for doctors to be Christian, employers to be Christian, lawyers to be Christian and so on. It may sound subtle but there is a world of difference. You see, what Jesus calls for, what he demands is for his followers to make, what one author called, "The Monday Connection"; to live what they profess on Sunday Monday through Saturday, each and every day of their life. Jesus knew that if those who call him Lord could only make "the Monday Connection" that they would revolutionize the world.

A brief word on Blameless. Blameless is a sacrificial word in Scripture. An animal offered for sacrifice would have to first be inspected to certify that it was without blemish--blameless. In places in this world where child sacrifice is still practiced by witch doctors--I saw this in Uganda--parents will intentionally scar their child to reduce the risk of kidnapping for these rituals.

In Ephesians when the writer said us that we are both holy and blameless he was saying that we need to offer the whole of our lives in service to God. And service to God is not a call to "professional ministry". It is a call to ministry in whatever profession or station you find yourself.

So, who do you think you are? Who do you think First Federated Church is? Well, I'll tell you the answer revealed in the baptismal font; you--we--are chosen before the foundation of the world to be both holy and blameless. We are called to embrace this gift called Life and to live it to the glory of God all of our days whether they be long or brief. Amen.

Fools for Christ

Mark 16: 1-8; John 20: 1-10; Luke 24: 1-12

Today is April Fool's Day, besides being Easter. The last time this occurred was in 1956. April Fool's Day is a day of pranks, hoaxes and good natured high-jinx. Its origin can be traced back to Chaucer's Canterbury Tales. If someone was unfamiliar with the Christian faith, they may think that the story of Easter is the biggest April Fool's joke ever. The disciples thought that the women's account was a "foolish tale". How many times have women been dismissed so callously over the centuries?

In his first letter to the Corinthians the apostle Paul wrote that the story of Easter is a stumbling block to some and foolishness to others. (I Corinthians 1:23) But this morning I want us to consider "Who's the biggest fool?" Maybe it is Pontius Pilate, the Roman governor. He could have stopped the crucifixion. By all indications he wanted to. After interrogating Jesus he said,

"I find no crime in this man". Besides, Pilate was a busy man and the ridiculous customs of the Jews was of no concern to him. Added to this was the troubling dream that his wife had concerning Jesus. She warned Pilate about getting involved with the controversy surrounding Jesus. (Matthew 27:19) But did he listen? No. Instead he listened to the crowd. Swayed by public opinion he was too weak to stand against it. So, he ceremonially washed his hands and declared that Jesus' blood not to be on his hands. His was far from a profile in courage. So history writes that the stain of Jesus' blood is on Pilate's hands. The stain of

Jesus is on all hands that ignore or are content with injustice. Injustice anywhere is injustice everywhere.

Maybe the bigger fool was Annas or his son-in-law Caiaphas. Annas was the high priest who loved the Temple and the "institution" more than he did the One to whom they pointed; namely God.

Caiaphas, on the other hand, feared a Roman backlash. He said that it was better for one man to die for the many than for the many to die for one man. If only he knew the truth of those words. It was Jesus who said that unless a grain of wheat falls into the earth, it remains but a single grain of wheat. But if it dies it produces many seeds. (John 12:24)

Consider the foolishness of the disciples. Where were they? Huddled together, afraid. After Jesus' arrest they scattered like sheep, just as Jesus said that they would. And Peter, the first to understand that Jesus was the Christ, denied him three times. None of the disciples were with the women at either the crucifixion or the tomb.

The story of Jesus, the story of Easter, does not end with either the Cross or the Grave. In the dawn's light the women saw the stone rolled away from the mouth of the tomb. In the cool damp air of the tomb they saw a "young man" dressed in a white robe sitting where Jesus had lain. "Don't be afraid," he said. "You are looking for Jesus the Nazarene, who was crucified.

He has risen! He is not here. See the place where they laid him? Go and tell his disciples and Peter, too. He is going ahead to Galilee where he will meet them.

But the women, trembling and bewildered, were afraid and told no one. Or did they? How else would we know the story? Fear may have its moments, but it never wins. It never has the last word.

Mark's original ending is unsatisfactory to many. The story seems incomplete. Subsequent followers added two different endings to the story; both a shorter and longer version. But I like the original both because of its starkness and its challenge. You see, the story of Easter is still being written. It did not end on that first Easter morning. The story of Easter ends with us,

with each one of us. The story of Easter calls us to be foolish enough to take Jesus seriously.

It demands that we fight injustice and prejudice, and bigotry, and hatred. It demands that we tear down the walls that separate and divide. It calls us to be strong. In the words of the letter of II Timothy, "God did not give us the spirit of timidity and fear, but of Power, and Love, and Self-Discipline.

By the power of God, we have been saved and called to a holy life--not because of anything we have done, but because of His own purpose and grace. This grace was given us in Christ Jesus before the beginning of time. It is time for us to live into that grace, that amazing grace. Amen.

A Way Out of No Way
Genesis 17: 1-16

Frizzel Gray, (you kind of wonder what mother would name her son "Frizzel", don't you?) grew up in one of the toughest neighborhoods in Baltimore, a section of the city known as "Turner's Corner". His single mother worked multiple jobs as she cared for her children and did the best, she could to keep them safe from the mean and alluring streets of the neighborhood. When times were particularly hard, she would encourage her children to have faith and remember that "God will find a way out of no way."

When Frizzel was sixteen his mother was diagnosed with cancer and died shortly thereafter leaving him and his sisters alone. Over the next six years he made several bad decisions. He dropped out of school and slowly succumbed to the values of the tough neighborhood streets. He became a street hustler and small-time thug. He mastered "the stare" and the pecking order needed for survival.

Then, when he was around 22 years old something happened that to this day, he finds it difficult to explain. He was shooting craps with his buddies in an alley on "Hankin's Corner", named by the neighborhood after a favorite liquor store. It was summer and the night was hot and muggy. Suddenly, Frizzel began to feel very odd, funny. In spite of the heat he suddenly chilled to the bone and his knees began to weaken. He slowly slid down the brick wall that he was leaning against into a sitting position. Voices went in and out. He began to lose his focus. And then a cloud began to suddenly come toward him, silently. As the cloud approached the chill left Frizzel's bones and was replaced by a strange comforting warmth. It was familiar. Where had he felt it before? Ah, when he was six years old. It was like the warmth of his mother. It was Love. He had forgotten what it felt like.

Then, in the midst of the cloud a face slowly took shape. As it came into view Frizzel recognized it as his mother's face. And she was looking intently at him with eyes that were so filled with sadness that it hurt. She saw what he had become, and she looked away a cosmic sense of sadness. Then she turned to him again with those eyes, but this time they were different. They were filled with Love.

Frizzel Gray vowed at that moment things would be different. He walked into that alley as Frizzel Gray, but he walked out of it as Kweisi Mfume, "son of conquering kings". In the subsequent years he received his G.E.D., a personality on a popular Baltimore radio station, a city councilman, a congressman, the president of the N.A.A.C.P., and is currently the chair of the board of regents of Morgan State University.

Today is the second in our Lenten sermon series on "covenants", a term that we do not use much in everyday language anymore. It is an agreement. Last week we explored the covenant that God made with Noah and all of Creation Forever and Ever. This week we look at the covenant between God and Abraham.

This is the second covenant that God made with Abraham. The first covenant came in chapter 12 of Genesis when God called

Abram, as he was then called, to leave his homeland and all that he knew to set off on a journey toward an unknown future armed only with faith in the One that called him. God promised protection, yet Abram was full of doubt. He wasn't sure that he could really trust this Voice, this God.

No sooner had he left his homeland than a famine ravaged the land. Abram went to Egypt in the hopes of finding relief from the famine. While there his wife Sarai caught the attention of Pharaoh who wished to add her to his household. Inquiries were made to Abram regarding Sarai, and Abram, fearful for his own life, lied and told Pharaoh that Sarai was his sister not his wife! It was only God's intervention that saved Sarai from being a permanent part of Pharaoh's household!

And then, later when it appeared that Sarai could not conceive, Abram and Sarai did things "their way" when Sarai gave Abram her handmaid Hagar as a surrogate mother. Abram took Hagar into his tent and she conceived ultimately bearing a son named Ishmael. Twice Abram's faith in the One who called him faltered.

God came to Abram once again with a new covenant, a renewed covenant. God gave Abram a new start, a "do over", if you will. The promise was reaffirmed. The sign of this covenant was circumcision, a reminder that God is always faithful, God always keeps promises. Their names were changed, Abram to Abraham and Sarai to Sarah. Sarah conceived and bore a son named Isaac.

Life happens, as we all know. Things do not always go as planned. Conflict arose between Hagar and Sarah because of their children. When Sarah asked Abraham to banish, "get that woman and her child out of her sight", Abraham was torn. He was torn between his affection to the mother of his first-born child and the mother of the child of the Promise. He was torn between his love for Ishmael and Isaac. Once again God spoke to Abraham and told him to do as his wife Sarah asked. Abraham asked for God's pledge that God would look after Ishmael and Hagar. God told Abraham that since Ishmael was the fruit of Abraham's loin, he was also a child of promise. God would take care of him and his mother. And God did, because God always keeps promises even when we mess things up.

And then later, in that horrible story that is so hard to unpack and understand, so hard to make sense of, the story that just tears at our hear, God asked Abraham to sacrifice his son Isaac. Abraham, not knowing how Isaac could be the child of the Promise and not understanding what God was doing, obeyed. Over the years he learned that God, in impossible situations, can "make a way out of no way." Abraham took Isaac to the mountain and prepared him for the sacrifice. At the last minute, as Abraham raised his knife, God once again intervened. A more suitable sacrifice was found, a ram caught in the brambles of the mountain. So together, Abraham and Isaac made the sacrifice.

In an episode of the television series, *Code Black,* one of the characters, a doctor, is told by a patient who is bravely facing death; "Humans want answers. But the answers that we need do not come with photographic evidence. They require you to believe in something you can't see. After all, that's why we call it faith. Otherwise we'd call it proof."

President Eisenhower once noted that planning is essential, but plans are worthless. We like to plan out our days and our hours and our lives. Sometimes we even like to plan the lives of others! (Bad idea, by the way.) But we also need to be open to the movement of God in our lives. In these remaining days of Lent I invite you to try this spiritual discipline. As you wake up take just a few seconds and silently ask God what God has planned for you today; what God wants you to do today. And then, go about your day, work through your checklists and your plans but when an interruption intrudes, silently ask yourself if this is God inviting you to do Kingdom work. Then as you lay down to sleep, briefly review the day in your mind that discover the "God moments" that came to you because you were open to God's Presence, God's Plans.

God can make a way out of no way. Amen.

True Religion
James 1: 17-27; Mark 7: 1-8, 15-15, 21-23

(True) religion that is pure and undefiled before God and the Father is this: to visit orphans and widows in their affliction, and to keep oneself unstained from the world.

Religion is falling out of favor in America today. More and more people identify themselves as "spiritual" but not "religious." There's nothing new or earthshattering in this. In his book Pandora's Seed, Spencer Wells noted that from dawn of humanity humans have been "spiritual". The earliest human burial sites, even before human history, indicate that humans had certain "rituals" that they used when someone died. Skeletal remains have trinkets and artifacts of something buried with them.

St. Augustine once wrote that our hearts are restless until they come in rest in God.

Religion does not deny spirituality. It grows out of spirituality. More and more people are searching past spiritual practices—religions—to give their spirituality shape.

So when someone says that they are spiritual but there not religious, what they are really saying is that the current tools of religion, Christian religion, generally, are not useful in understanding their spirituality.

The problem with religion is that it can become like great-grandmother's Easter ham recipe. ....

The reason for the religious practice is lost. And, since nature abhors a vacuum, people develop traditions that eventually lose their voice in shaping spirituality. The tradition becomes that sacred.

This is essentially what happened in our gospel lesson. The Pharisees and the scribes saw that the disciples ate with unwashed hands, thus defiling themselves in the dominant Jewish custom of the day.

I have to say a word about the Pharisees and the scribes. I wonder if they are very happy. I mean, have you ever noticed how they always seem to be following Jesus and his disciples, finding fault, nitpicking, trying to start an argument, trying "to stir things up"? Do you think that they were happy? Have you ever known someone who is constantly nitpicking, finding fault, stirring things up as being happy? As soon as they "fix" one problem another problem always seems to crop up. That's how it seems to be with the Pharisees. With one exception, Jesus and his disciples never seem to be able to do anything right.

Anyway, the Pharisees and the scribes were wrong in their interruption of Jewish religion. The command of washing your hands before eating is found in Leviticus and only applies to the priest offering sacrifice in the Temple. They applied it to everyone by taking a different part of their scripture and saying that the nation was to be a priestly nation.

Jesus countered their criticism by pointing out that they sure are good at seeing the log in someone else's eye while being totally blind to the speck of sawdust in their own.

"How right the prophet Isaiah was when he spoke of you self-righteous hypocrites saying, 'They may honor me with their lips, but their hearts are far away. Their worship is vain because they teach as doctrine human precepts." They teach as "rules" their own "prejudices" and bias.

Jesus went on to point out that they worry themselves over a little handwashing ceremony, —because it wasn't for sanitation purposes, they knew nothing of germ theory. Washing your hands could simply be nothing more that pouring a little water over your hands—they worry about a handwashing ceremony and totally ignore a far weightier "tradition", that of respecting their elders by taking care of them in their old age.

The religion that the Pharisees and the scribes laid upon the people was a shadow image of spirituality that was alive. Indeed, on a different occasion in a different gospel Jesus said that the Pharisees were like white washed tombs—looking all pristine on the outside but dead and rotting on the inside.

Keeping religion relevant to spirituality is a constant challenge, even in the early church. Within a generation James wrote the letter that bears his name.

"True religion that is pure and undefiled before God is this: to visit the orphans and widows in their affliction, and to keep oneself unstained from the world."

The orphaned and the widowed were the bottom two rungs on society's ladder. The orphaned had no one. All they could do to survive was beg, steal or sell themselves into prostitution or slavery.

The widowed were one step above the orphaned because they had more resources and more options—though, not many—to survive.

Eugene Peterson in *The Message* renders it like this: Real religion, the kind that passes muster before God the Father, is this: Reach out to the homeless and forgotten, and guard against the corruption of the world.

In other words, care for those who are neglected, defend those who have no earthly defender and corruption.

James went on to say that if we are hearers of the word—the word of God—but do not do anything about it—in other words, there is no visible reflection of the word in your life—you're only deceiving yourself. My wife has said on multiple occasions that someone should not be surprised to learn that you attend church.

People who take Jesus seriously "bridle" their tongue. Words have power, they have meaning. Many a friendship, many a relationship, many a marriage have been destroyed by words, said in anger, said in jest, said without thinking.

A true religion changes things. It changes our hearts. It changes our actions. It changes what we say. It changes how we treat one another and most importantly, how we treat the least the last and the lost.

James challenges us to live up to our baptism, our calling.

It has been said that if you cannot be a good example, at least be a good warning. James wants us to be good examples so that others may see our good works and give glory to God in heaven.

Amen.

Sugar for the Soul
Luke 6: 17-26, Jeremiah 17: 56-10, Psalm 1

Blessed are those who trust in the Lord for they shall be like trees planted near a stream. (Jeremiah 17: 7&8)

Blessings and woes. I like blessings. I'm not so fond of woes. They scare me. A variation of today's lesson also appears in Matthew's gospel as a part of the Sermon on the Mount. It begins that sermon with what is commonly called the "Beatitudes" --the blessings. I like those better. I like to be blessed. I don't like to be judge me. Please, don't judge me.

The gospel lesson assigned for today in the common lectionary is Luke's version of Jesus' teaching, and it contains uncomfortable contrasts between the "blessings" and the "woes". I believe that we are often tempted to "tame" the teaching the teachings of Jesus, especially when they challenge us. Such is the case with today's lesson. We are sorely tempted to take the sting out of Jesus' words and comfort ourselves by saying that there is some kind of virtue in poverty. But if you ever experienced poverty, or uncomfortable want, or even mild want, for that matter, you know that poverty is not a virtue. There is nothing virtuous in poverty No one aspires to poverty. Poverty is not something that we wish for our children.

I think that at times we who are surrounded by plenty try to ease our conscience by saying that the poor are somehow "closer to God" than the rest of us. After all, didn't Jesus himself say the poor are "blessed". But if they are "closer" to God it is because God is all they have to hang on to.

In today's gospel lesson Jesus did not commend poverty or hunger or want. But neither did He condemn wealth. Rather he challenged us to take a closer look at our spiritual health in light of our wealth--for we are wealthy by the world's standard. Jesus invited us to think about the real source of security. What really makes us secure?

I believe that we have a gnawing hunger within our very being named "Security". Its alias is "Desire". We constantly seek ways to satisfy this hunger. Advertisers know this and feed our soul hunger. They tempt us with "sugar for the soul" which may satisfy us now but ultimately leaves craving more.

I will give you an example of what I am talking about. In her book *My Turn*, the late Ruth Bell Graham told the story of a time when her son, Ned, was at the age when he wanted a bicycle more than anything. He had been playing with his friend Joel Baker, and he wanted a bicycle just like Joel's. His father, Billy Graham told him to wait until Christmas, but Christmas was such a long time away. Ned shared his lament with Joel. Joel decided to lend Ned his bike for a week. In the course of that week Ned realized that Joel's bike would be too small for him by Christmas. So, he upped the ante. Now he had to have a larger ten-speed bike.

But even the love affair didn't last until Christmas! In the mail appeared the annual Sears & Roebuck Christmas catalog. Some of you are old enough to remember the excitement of receiving the Sears & Roebuck Christmas catalog. It was a world of wonder and a source of many a child's "wish list". Well, in the catalog Ned saw the "perfect" bike. It had a banana seat, three-speed stick shift, and butterfly handlebars--some of you remember those--and slicks! It was every young boy's dream! But Christmas was still a couple of months away! I do not know if that was the bicycle that he settled on or how long it satisfied him, but the "things" of this world do not satisfy. They are "sugar for the soul". And this is where the "woes" come into play.

We feel financially insecure and constantly build "bigger barns". We save for a "rainy day" but we can't recognize a "rainy day "even when we are standing in knee high in water. We spend our lives chasing "enough" but "enough" is always just beyond our reach. We say that we are not rich or wealthy because we believe that rich people always have ten percent more than we have. That's the problem with thing; they are with shiny objects that lead us down paths of distraction and destruction. This story is as old as humanity, the Garden of Eden, and older than the Odyssey, with the hypnotizing song of the Sirens.

In contrast to this, God wants us to be rooted in a faith that can sustain us, even in a time of hardship and famine. Jeremiah contrasted those who put their trust in themselves and in this world saying that they are like desert plants withering on salt plains. Those who trust in the Lord are like trees planted near a free-flowing stream, sinking deep roots and producing sweet fruit).

The Psalmist sang of the "happiness" of living in God's shadow. (I like to use the word "sing" rather than "said" for two reasons; one, the Psalms were written as song, and secondly, there is an unquenchable power in music and song. Let me write the song, a Scottish covenanter said, and I will lead the nation.)

"Happiness," Pamela Coutre wrote is complex and not easily achieved. Happiness or blessedness is not found in facades, goods, achievements, or accolades. Happiness is an "inside job". It is found in a contented heart. Abraham Lincoln was once asked about an unhappy neighbor who was moving to a new community. "Do you think he'll be any happier there?" someone asked Lincoln. "Well," Lincoln replied, "I reckon that he'll be as happy as he makes up his mind to be."

Woes are transformed into blessings in the spiritual disciplines of worship, prayer, fellowship, stewardship and mission.

Happy are those whose delight is in the Lord.

Blessed are those who trust in the Lord for they shall be like trees planted near a stream.

Where have you planted your life.?

Amen.

Relationship Over Revenge

Genesis 45: 3-11, 15; Psalm 37: 1-7; I Corinthians 15: 35-38, 42-50; Luke 6: 27-38

But I say to you that listen, Love your enemies, do good to those who hate you. (v. 27)

One of the biggest decisions that have to make in life, a decision that will affect our happiness more than any other decision is this; do we seek relationships over revenge?

At a time when Palestine was occupied by the imperial might of ancient Rome, when the Pax Romana or "Roman Peace" demanded unquestioned obedience and was maintained by brutal oppression, when dissenters were executed by the most brutal of means known to humanity, crucifixion, a humiliating death designed to intimidate much like the ISIS beheadings of today, the words of Jesus were startling. One might even say that they were naive.

In spite of all of this, Jesus saw a new world where, a world that the prophets of old envisioned, a world where the lion would lie down with the lamb, the child would play over the den of the adder, spears would be turned into pruning hooks, swords into plowshares, and all of God's children would live in harmony. This alternative way sought relationships over revenge.

An eye for an eye and a tooth for a tooth may seem just but it was actually empty. As Martin Luther King, Jr. observed, "If we do an eye for an eye and a tooth for a tooth, we will be a blind and toothless nation."

We have no written record of Jesus' thought process. We know that he was raised in a family who instilled the habit of worship in his heart. He regularly sang the Psalms, for they were the hymns written for worship. He would have heard the stories of his people and informed by the wisdom of the prophets. One of the Psalms that he would have sung was our Call to Worship, Psalm 37.

Do not fret because of those who are evil or be envious of those who do wrong; for they are like grass that soon withers, like green plants that soon die. … Trust in the Lord and do good.

His temptation gave Jesus the opportunity to "trust in the way of the Lord" as nothing else could. And, I believe that he knew the story of Joseph, one of my favorite characters in the Old Testament because of his resilience. Joseph was not only resilient but a dreamer, or perhaps, better understood as a person with a gift. He had night visions, dreams that one day he would be an important figure in the life of his family. But rather than keep these dreams to himself, he shared them with his family. His older brothers grew tired of his dreams in which he was also "the special one." Their father Jacob didn't help matters. He showed blatant favoritism to Joseph. He even gave him a precious coat of "many colors", in some translations, or with "long sleeves" in other translations.

In any case, the brothers grew tired of him. In the youthful lack of good judgment and the abundant impulsiveness that males are known for possessing, they conspired to kill him by taking his special coat and throwing him into a pit to die. Perhaps out of "second thoughts" or maybe, making a little profit on the side, one of the brothers convinced the others to sell Joseph to a caravan bound for Egypt. The thinking seemed to have been that his "blood" wouldn't be on their hands. They covered their tracks by dipping his coat in blood, presented it their father, and acted all sorrowful as they related to how Joseph had been killed by a lion. Thus, began Joseph's long journey from the pit of despair to the crown.

Joseph was sold to an Egyptian named Potiphar. Potiphar soon recognized Joseph's intelligence and unshakable honesty. Potiphar put him in charge of his household. Now, while Potiphar could trust Joseph without question, his wife was another matter. She had a roving amorous eye. Not accustomed to having her advances rejected, her unrequited advances toward Joseph left her embarrassed. Afraid of what her husband would do it he heard about her propositions, she made up a story about Joseph, one that landed him in prison, most likely awaiting execution.

In prison Joseph's leadership shined once again. He was taken off of death row and put in charge of a section of the prison. He still had visions and gained some renown as an interpreter of dreams. Eventually word of his gift for interpreting dreams reached Pharaoh for the monarch had two recurrent and troubling dreams.

Pharaoh sent for Joseph who was not only able to interpret the dreams but developed a "game plan" as well. Joseph told

Pharaoh that Egypt would experience seven years of abundant harvest and seven years of drought. In order to avoid famine, grain needed to be stored for the lean years to come. So impressed was Pharaoh with Joseph that Joseph became Pharaoh's most trusted adviser, second only to Pharaoh himself.

When the famine arrived Jacob, Joseph's father, sent Joseph's older brothers to Egypt in search of relief. Joseph recognized his brothers immediately, but they did not recognize him. Why would they? They may have thought that Joseph was dead, but even if he wasn't, this was the last place they expected him. I wonder if from time to time they were haunted by their action, especially whenever their father would grow sad and quiet around the time of Joseph's birth or that awful day when he heard the news of Joseph's death.

In any event, there came a day for the "big reveal". And Joseph had to decide if he would relationship or revenge? Here's what happened next.

Joseph said to his brothers, "I am Joseph. Is my father still alive?" But his brothers could not answer him. They were stunned. Could this really be Joseph? Alive? After all of these years? How?

Then Joseph said to his brothers, "Come closer to me. I am your brother, Joseph, whom you sold into Egypt. I can just imagine what was going on through their minds. Can't you? Oh no, this can't be happening. But then Joseph said something totally unexpected. He decided if he valued relationship or revenge more. I like to think his decision touched Jesus' heart when he was told the story of this patriarch.

Joseph said, "Do not be distressed or angry with yourselves, because you sold me here; for God sent me before you to preserve life. ... God sent me before you to preserve for you a remnant on earth, and to keep alive for you many survivors. So it was not you who sent me here, but God; God has made me a father to Pharoah, and lord of all his house and ruler over all the land of Egypt. ... I will provide for you. Otherwise you and your household and all who belong to you will become destitute. ...

"Tell my father all about the honor accorded me in Egypt and bring him here quickly. "Then he threw his arms around his brother Benjamin and wept. And Benjamin wept, too. "And he kissed all his brothers and wept over them. And they talked."

In his letter to the Corinthian church the apostle Paul invited serious Jesus followers to surround themselves with the things that represent God's Kingdom. Hate, jealousy, exploitation, these are the things that cause suffering and harm. The teachings of Jesus show us a society that represents God's Kingdom. Love, Peace, Forgiveness, Justice.

You see, Jesus pointed to a radical paradigm shift in which one gives up their right to revenge. Jesus presented the world with an alternative to "the harsh reality" of the world. Rather than entering into a mode of escalating violence which leads to more and more death, Jesus told his apostles, disciples and even the "crowd", to do something radical.

Love your enemies and do good to those who hate you.

People who take Jesus seriously know a generous God and therefore they can be generous themselves. They know a forgiving God and can therefore be forgiving.

I invite you to listen again to today's gospel lesson; this time as the late Eugene Peterson, pastor, theologian, and writer rendered our Savior's words.

"To you who are ready for the truth, I say this: Love your enemies. Let them bring out the best in you, not the worst. When someone gives you a hard time, respond with the energies of prayer for that person. If someone slaps you in the face, stand there and take it. If someone grabs your shirt, giftwrap your best coat and make a present of it. If someone takes unfair advantage of you, use the occasion to practice the servant life. No more tit-for-tat stuff. Live generously. Here is a simple rule of thumb for behavior: Ask yourself what you want people to do for you; then grab the initiative and do it for them! If you only love the lovable, do you expect a pat on the back? Run-of-the-mill sinners do that. If you only help those who help you, do you expect a medal? Garden-variety sinners do that. If you only give for what you hope to get out of it, do you think that's charity? The stingiest of pawnbrokers does that. I tell you, love your enemies. Help and give without expecting a return. You'll never—I promise—regret it. Live out this God-created identity the way our Father lives toward us, generously and graciously, even when we're at our worst. Our Father is kind; you be kind. Don't pick on people, jump on their failures, criticize their faults—unless, of course, you want the same treatment. Don't condemn those who are down; that hardness can boomerang. Be easy on people; you'll find life a lot easier. Give away your life; you'll find life given back, but not merely given back—given back with bonus and blessing. Giving, not getting, is the way. Generosity begets generosity."

So, what's it going to be in your life; relationship or revenge?

To God be the glory. Amen.

The God Who Embraced Me

Psalm 147: 1-11, 20c

John W. Fountain talking about an "Abba" God in his life said,

"I believe in God. Not that cosmic, intangible spirit-in-the-sky that Mama told me as a little boy "always was and always will be." But the God who embraced me when Daddy disappeared from our lives — from my life at age four — the night police led him away from our front door, down the stairs in handcuffs.

The God who warmed me when we could see our breath inside our freezing apartment, where the gas was disconnected in the dead of another wind-whipped Chicago winter, and there was no food, little hope and no hot water.

The God who held my hand when I witnessed boys in my 'hood swallowed by the elements, by death and by hopelessness; who claimed me when I felt like "no-man's son," amid the absence of any man to wrap his arms around me and tell me, "everything's going to be okay," to speak proudly of me, to call me son.

I believe in God, God the Father, embodied in his Son Jesus Christ. The God who allowed me to feel His presence — whether by the warmth that filled my belly like hot chocolate on a cold afternoon, or that voice, whenever I found myself in the tempest of life's storms, telling me (even when I was told I was "nothing") that I was something, that I was His, and that even amid the desertion of the man who gave me his name and DNA and little else, I might find in Him sustenance.

I believe in God, the God who I have come to know as father, as Abba — Daddy.

*****

So who is this God that John Fountain came to know as "Abba; the God whose warmth filled his belly "like hot chocolate on a cold afternoon"? It is the One who knows the number of the stars in an ever-expanding infinite Universe; the One who broke the Darkness of Creation with Light before throwing the sun, the moon, and the stars against the heavens.

It is the One who heals the brokenhearted and continues to bind up the wounds of the wounded. That's a big God but a God that is not so big that He does not care for each and every one of us. It is a God who listens to the smallest and most mundane prayer as well as the gut-wrenching cry of a broken soul.

A woman once confessed to her minister (not me) that she feared she "misused" God. As you can imagine, all kinds of thoughts when through the minister's head. What could she have possibly done?" "What was she about to confess?" "Can you ever really 'misuse' God?" Bracing herself, the minister invited to parishioner to go on. It seems that the woman couldn't find her car keys one morning for the life of her. She searched high and low; her purse,

the nightstand beside her bed. She even searched in the refrigerator--she tended to be easily distracted--but no luck. Finally, she said a little prayer asking God to help her find her keys. And you know what? within minutes she remembered that the last time she used her keys she was wearing a little worn coat. She checked the coat pocket and sure enough! she found the keys!

"God's got a whole lot of more important things to worry about then my keys," she continued.

"Nonsense," the minister replied. "If God cares for the sparrow, God certainly cares for you and your lost keys."

God's cares for us is like the love a good daddy has for his children. God loves us like an attentive mother loves her nursing child. Our Psalm reminds us that God only threw the stars into the heavens but knows their number. Such knowledge is whole and complete. It is, I believe, what Paul meant when he wrote, "For now we see in a mirror, dimly, but then we will see face to face. Now I know only in part; then I will know fully, even as I have been fully known. (I Corinthians 13: 12)

The Psalm also tells us that God is cloaked not in a Harry Potter "cloak of invisibility", but in unfathomable mystery. This mystery, though, is not impenetrable, though. In my office I have a quote from my father that I found after his death. "My variety of Christianity", he wrote, "is not used to explain everything. It accepts and appreciates (the) mystery."

God's unfathomable mystery is what theologians call Transcendence. The word itself literally means "to surpass". It refers to the "Otherness" of God. Many years ago J.B. Phillips wrote a little book entitled *Your God Is Too Small*. In it he expressed how we try to shrink God into our understanding.

C.S. Lewis wrote about this in his "Chronicles of Narnia". In the first book, *The Lion, the Witch, and the Wardrobe*, the children, Peter, Susan, Edmund and Lucy ask if the lion Aslan, the God figure, is safe. Their question is met with shock and surprise. "Safe? No, he's not safe…but he's good. He's the King." (The Lion, the Witch and the Wardrobe, chapter 8, "What Happened After Dinner)

God is not limited to what our minds can conceive, nor is God's Goodness confined to our understanding of Goodness. The psalmist marveled that God is neither bound by human frailty, nor stymied by human limits.

This Table, the communion table, and the sacrament that we are about to participate in reminds us that our God is big enough to care, for lost keys, lost souls, hungry children, homeless children, refugees and country club members alike and all at the same time.

God cares for each of us equally, and invites those who take Jesus seriously to care for

the least, the last and lost, too. God is present in the day to day activities of our lives. God is both Transcendent and Immanent, or within us. It is this God who John W. Fountain, like Jesus, called "Abba", father. It is this God who we can call "Abba", too. Amen.

Simple Math

James 3: 13-4:3, 7-8

Who is wise and understanding among you? Show by your good life that your works are done with gentleness born of wisdom. (v. 13)

I drove back from Chicago last night after making a hospital visit at the University of Illinois Hospital, Chicago in the morning and being my wife's "arm candy" at an evening wedding. While finding my way from the Homewood-Flossmoor area of Chicagoland to my home I followed my Waze GPS. In the dark hours before driving home and finally free of the Chicago area traffic I began to wonder about the "little man" who resides in my GPS and does such a good job guiding me home. Of course, there is no little man but an algorithm doing all the work. Algorithms, as you may know are a finite number of steps with frequent repetition of steps to solve a problem. They are used nearly everywhere--from GPS to web searches and all things in between.

We've been looking at the letter of James. Some people say that the epistle is a counterbalance to Paul's emphasis on Faith. But that was not James' intent. Although he would not have known the word, James gives us a faith algorithm. To James, Faith and Works goes hand in hand. "Show me your works," he said earlier in this epistle, "and I will show you your Faith." James algorithm is Faith + Works = Wisdom. Who is wise and understanding among you? Show by your good life that your works are done with gentleness born of wisdom.

Jesus said something very similar. He told his disciples to be "wise as serpents and innocent as doves." By that he meant that we must know the way that the world works without adopting the ways of the world.

The ways of the world and the ways of the Kingdom I believe can be best illustrated by looking at two real life examples. Simon Sinek is a business consultant, author and lecturer. He recently noted that today's standardized business models are left overs from the 1980s and '90s. Those were largely boom years in the United States. The Berlin Wall fell, and the Soviet Union broke apart. One author said that we were at the end of history as he did not foresee anything that could threaten Western liberal democracy. Of course, this was naive, as recent events illustrate.

In the 1980s and '90s the standardized business model became "shareholder supremacy". The needs of the shareholders took precedence over the needs of workers and the society in general. As a consequence many businesses-maintained shareholder dividends by laying off workers to cut costs. Their "worldview" went from long range to quarterly. Sinek said that this is like a coach trying to build up a strong team by prioritizing the needs of the fans over the needs of the players. This unbalanced corporate culture led to the primary means of incentivizing people through bonuses which led investment banks to literally create environments where all employees became addicted to numbers. This led to cutting ethical and legal corners to get a bonus and feel valued.

This is not the way that capitalism is designed to work. The basic structure of capitalism is that if you take care of people the people will take care of the business. But when numbers become more important than the people and people become expendable the result is that trust is eroded, and employees no longer look out for the company but for themselves. Years of goodwill and trust can be destroyed almost overnight and it takes 20-30 years to reestablish that goodwill.

Contrast this business model with a different one. In the recession of 2008 Barry-Wehmiller was a US company with about three billion dollars in revenue and 8000 employees. When the recession hit, almost overnight, they lost thirty percent of their orders. The company's board of directors want to have mass layoffs, but CEO Bob Chapman was committed to "his people". He resisted the knee-jerk reaction and took a different approach. He implemented a furlough program whereby every employee had to take four weeks of unpaid vacation. They could do this whenever they wanted to do it and they did not have to take the weeks consecutively. When he announced the program to the employees, he said that it was better that everyone suffers a little rather than have a few suffer a lot. As Sinek tells the story, morale shot up as did production. The employees felt safe as opposed to disposable and company loyalty is second to none. There is nothing that the employees wouldn't do for the company because they feel valued.

Wisdom is when Faith and Works go together like a hand in a glove. Wisdom doesn't see "either/or", "black or white". Wisdom looks for a third way, a better way, the Kingdom way-- all for the glory of God. Amen.

Wind and Fire
Joel 2:28

The manse, or parsonage, in our first call was a roomy ranch-style home that sat on 3 acres, 3 miles outside of a town of 350 in Warren County, Illinois. While there we got a taste and an appreciation of country living. I bought a pair of "chore boots" from the Farm King and was laughed at the first time I wore them to hog lot. I was awakened at 2 in the morning to watch a farmer "pull a calf". I became familiar with the sweet dusty aroma of the town's feed store. We had a "burn barrel" near our vegetable garden on the west side of the yard. Under two large acorn trees wild asparagus grew in the spring. It was the first time I had ever eaten asparagus.

Being city slickers getting into the lifestyle of rural America we noticed that many people "burned off" their gardens in the fall. One afternoon we decided to burn off our garden. We pulled out our 250 feet of garden hose and set fire to the garden. Before long we heard the crackling of dried plants as ghostly smoke rose into the air.

A little while after we started the fire an unexpected autumn blew in from the north. The lazy fire perked up and grew in intensity. Small flames of debris floated up heavenward straight toward our fence line and a dry cornfield waiting to be harvested. Sue manned the hose while I ran from spark to spark stomping out new little fires. All the while I couldn't help but to think of what people would say if the cornfield went ablaze.

Fortunately the corn field didn't go up in smoke. We put the fire out. And I learned that wind and fire are a dangerous combination. They are dangerous because you cannot control them. They have a mind of their own. They can destroy, but they can also bring about new beginnings.

Pentecost is a sign of new beginnings. On the day of Pentecost, our lesson says, when the faithful were gathered together in one place, a sound like a mighty wind swept through the place and tongues like fire danced above the disciple's heads. Each were able to speak as they never had before. And people who came to Jerusalem from the corners of the known world--Parthians and Medes, residents of Mesopotamia, Judea and Egypt, visitors from Rome, both Jews and proselytes, new converts--heard about God's mighty power and amazing love in their own native tongue.

Last week I was the guest of a colleague at the Southside Mission's annual banquet in the Peoria Civic Center ballroom. A sold-out event attended by about 1000 people heard the Rev. John Perkins--a civil rights leader turned best-selling author deliver the keynote address. At 88 he came to the stage with a very unsteady gait, one that made me quite nervous. But as he spoke, the years seemed to peel off of his shoulders and his voice became steadier.

As a young man he was beaten near death by an angry mob of white folks. As he lay in his hospital room, he hated all white people. But then he looked around at the white doctors and nurses who cleaned his wound and were so kind and caring. He realized that there were "good" white people and "bad" white people. His "conversion moment", though, came when his young son came home from "Good News Club" singing a little song that he learned that day. He sang the little song over and over again.

"Jesus loves the little children,
All the children of the world;
Red and yellow, black and white
They are precious in His sight
Jesus loves the little children of the world.

Quoting from his most recent book, *Do All Lives Matter? The Issues We Can No Longer Ignore and the Solutions We All Long For,* the Rev. Jenkins said that the question of whether black lives matter is "an insane question. ... All lives matter."

"God never wanted people to ask that question," he continued. "(The question) shows the misery in our society. (It) shows how much we dislike each other's. We are of one blood. There is no such thing as a black race or a white race or a yellow race or a red race; there is only the human race."

We are so good, so adept, so skilled at focusing on our differences that we are blind to that which binds us together. Pentecost presents us with a new day. It seems to me that the challenge that Pentecost lays before our feet is one to tearing down the walls that divide us. Perkins challenged those in attendance last Monday night to "Listen. Listen. Listen. Listen. ... We need each other. ... Listening is prayer. Prayer is hope; prayer is expectation." Prayer is redemptive.

Speaking through the Old Testament prophet Joel God said,

"In the last days I will pour out my Spirit upon all flesh,
and your sons and your daughters will prophesy,
and your young men shall see visions,
while your old men shall dream dreams.
Even upon the lowliest I will pour out my Spirit;
and they shall prophesy."

With Pentecost a new chapter is dawning; a new chapter is being penned in our lives. Are we up to the challenge of tearing down walls, of being color blind, and to see the face of God in the faces of the least, the last, the lost and the lonely?

Amen.

A Promise is a Promise: God Keeps Promises

Genesis 9: 8-17

At the end of this past Thursday's Lutheran Hillside Village bible study on today's Old Testament, one of the members of the class asked if he could share a story. It went something like this.

When Noah lowered the gangplank of the ark, he told all of the animals to "Go forth and multiply!" They left the ark two by two. As Noah was cleaning up, he saw two snakes coiled in the corner. "" Didn't you hear me?" Noah asked. "I said, 'Go forth and multiply!'" One of the snakes began to cry. "We can't go forth and multiply; we adders!"

The story of Noah, the Ark and the Rainbow are familiar but the theology behind the story, the symbolism, is less familiar.

Today we begin a sermon series on "Covenants" in the bible. "Covenant" is a word that isn't used much. The first time that I heard the word "covenant" was when my folks bought some land on which to build their house. The president of the homeowners' association came by asking them to sign a "covenant", an agreement about who they would, or importantly, would not sell their land and house to.

Covenants are like a "contract." As you may know, the offer, the acceptance, the intent, and consideration, or something of value, usually money.

The covenant of the Rainbow is not a two-party contract, but a forever promise that God made to all Creation, including humanity, you and me, all our ancestors, as well as all our heirs. So, what's the "backstory"?

The world that God created out of Chaos and called good, was devolving back to Chaos. First there was the so-called "Fall". Then there was the fratricide of Able. And on it went; the "celestial" sons of God took the daughters of earth as their wives thus compromising the proper relationship between heaven and earth. Violence and corruption increased exponentially. There seemed to be no end in sight, and it grieved God deeply. So God decided to "destroy the destroyers", to wipe the slate clean with a "watery chaos" in which all flesh would die.

But then God had second thoughts. God decided to save a "remanent." God is like that, you know. God always leaves a remnant, a chance for a "new beginning". In this new beginning, though, God renew that some things never change. What one person called "the law of the tooth and the claw" was not would not go away. The strong would always be tempted to overpower the weak.

When the flood waters finally receded and this "new generation" stepped forward, God realized that retribution never changes anything, especially the human heart. Nor does punishment coerce us into ultimately changing our ways. There is only one thing that is powerful enough to do that: Love.

In the closing scenes of the movie "Wonder Woman" Diana Prince says reflectively,

"I used to want to save the world; to end war and bring peace to mankind. But then, I glimpsed the darkness that lives within their light. I learned that inside every one of them, there will always be both. The choice each must make for themselves - something no hero will ever defeat. I've touched the darkness that lives in between the light. Seen the worst of this world, and the best. Seen the terrible things men do to each other in the name of hatred, and the lengths they'll go to for love. Now I know. Only love can save this world."

In the story of Noah and the Rainbow we see God turn from vindication to forgiveness, from frustration to patience. As one commentator said, "The creatures made in the image of God may always resist God, but God decided to "lay down" the Divine arsenal."

This first covenant, the Rainbow Covenant, was recorded at a time when the people of Israel were in exile from their land. The community was in chaos. We know what chaos is in our own time and place. We know it in our personal lives; relationships broken by death, personal illness, estrangement from those whom we love, or a feeling of estrangement from our community. The loss of a job or a home, or a way of life.

We know it in our communities; the death of seventeen people in a Florida high school, the death of fifty-eight people at a concert in Las Vegas, terrorism at home and overseas, wars that seem to know no end, natural disasters.

The list seems endless. It is endless.

But then we remember the story of Noah and the rainbow and tell it to our children and grandchildren, paint the story upon their walls and make mobiles because within that story there is a light of hope that shines brightly even in life's darkest hours.

God is faithful, even when we are not. God is with us, even when we feel alone. God will never forget us; God will always be with us to the very end of time and beyond.

Amen.

Roots and Wings
John 17:1-15

> *"Holy Father, protect them that they be one as we are one. ..."* (vs. 1)

> *"I am not asking you to take them out of the world, but I ask you to protect them from the evil one."* (vs. 15)

It has been said that there are two lasting things that we give our children; one is roots and the other is wings. Good deep roots make a good foundation upon which they build their lives.

Jesus once said that everyone who hears his words and does them will be like a wise man who built his house on the rock. When the rain falls, the floods come, and the winds blow beating on that house, it does not fall, because it had been built on rock. But those who hear his words and does not do them are like a foolish man who built his house on the sand. And when the rain fell, and the floods came, and the winds blew his house fell, "and great was the fall of it." (Matthew 7:24-27)

Wings give freedom and the courage to fly, to soar on the winds of life. Once again, Jesus said, "I have come that they might have life and have it abundantly." (John 10:10)

I was blessed with a mother and father who did their best to give me deep roots and strong wings. While they were not perfect parents, no parent is, they did their best to keep me grounded while giving me the freedom to fail. They set limits without to being controlling. They didn't try to "protect" me from the world. After dinner we would watch the evening news with either Walter Cronkite or Huntley and Brinkley. They never sent me out of the room or told me to close my eyes and not look at some story on the news. They took time to explain things to me that I could not otherwise understand. By today's standards they were probably too lenient but I suspect that they seemed to sense that I was going to face, in the word of that balladeer from an earlier time, Cat Stevens, that I would be walking into a "wild world where it is hard to get by just upon a smile."

This morning's gospel lesson is Jesus' attempt at giving his disciples a final lesson in "roots and wings". He was not to be with them much longer. The reading is part of what is called Jesus' "high priestly prayer". It occurred on the last night that he was with his disciples. Unlike the synoptic gospels of Matthew, Mark, and Luke, in John's gospel Jesus does not struggle with indecision. There is no prayer in the Garden of Gethsemane where Jesus wrestled with "the cup"; "if it be possible let this cup pass...but thy will be done". In John's gospel Jesus calmly walked to the Garden of Gethsemane for his arrest.

In this prayer, Jesus is at peace with himself and with God. In John's gospel the struggle for Jesus soul occurred in chapter 12; "Now my soul is troubled, and what shall I say" 'Father, save me from this hour'? No, it was for this very reason that I came to this hour." (v. 27)

In this prayer Jesus is preparing his disciples for what is to come. And he prayed for two things. First, that his disciples, then and now, "be one". I have often thought that it is neither idle hands nor idle minds that are the devil's playgrounds, but a church that is fully committed to the work of the Kingdom of God. Nothing strikes fear in the heart of the devil than a church hitting on all cylinders. The parable that Jesus told about "the enemy" sowing weeds in the night in a field of grain is a story of disharmony within the body of Christ.

When individuals allow the mantle of Christian leadership to be placed upon their shoulders, they vow to promote the "peace", "unity", and "purity" of the church for the church is called to be sign to the world of what God intends for all humanity. The terms peace, unity and purity are often misunderstood.

Peace is not simply the absence of conflict. Peace can only be known when we face our differences openly with the confidence that it is Jesus Christ, and Christ alone, that holds us together. We can do this because we know that Christ alone is the head of the church. Our diversity in temperament, background and culture are not something to be feared but something to be cherished. Everyone has a part to play in the body of Christ. But peace cannot come about when we are afraid, when some rule by intimidation or when everyone privately pretends to agree but in reality, feel isolated or unheard. Such peace comes at the expense of integrity and honesty.

Unity is fragile.

Unity doesn't mean "uniformity".

It means that there is a basic respect for one another whereby each person believes that the other is genuinely seeking to be faithful of Jesus Christ to the best of their ability. And it means that we, too, are seeking to be faithful to Jesus Christ.

Peace and unity are always in tension with "purity".

Purity does not come from uniformity or from narrow legalism but from seeking together to be faithful in the knowledge that we are but hewers of wood and drawers of water, stewards of God's Creation and servants in God's Kingdom that knows no end.

And that brings us to the second thing that Jesus prayed for in today's lesson; that God not take His disciples out of the world but protect--watch over them--as they engage in the world.

There is a scene in the Whoopi Goldberg movie "Sister Act" where Ms Goldberg portrayed a murder witness under protective custody in a Roman Catholic motherhouse and disguised as "Sister Mary Clarence" recruits the Monsignor O'Hara to encourage the Reverend Mother to allow the nuns in her charge to go out into the neighborhood. When the nuns here the news they are excited. "This is why I became a nun," one exclaims. There is so much good that we can do out there," another adds.

"But surely you know, Monsignor," the Reverend Mother sputtered, "how dangerous the neighborhood is."

"And you shall meet the danger," the Monsignor says with smiling confidence, and adds, "as if I could stop you!"

Jesus did not pray for his followers to be "safe".

He prayed for them to be "faithful".

He did not call them to "save" themselves, but to give themselves away."

On the front of today's bulletin there is a prayer from the Rev. Phillips Brooks.

O, do not pray for easy lives,
Pray to be stronger!
Do not pray for tasks equal to your powers.
Pray for powers equal to your tasks!
Then the doing of your work shall be no miracle.
But you shall be a miracle.
Every day you shall wonder at yourself,
as the richness of life which has come to you by the grace of God.
May that be our prayer, too.
Mothers, thank you for giving us roots and wings. Amen.

Written on the Heart
Jeremiah 31: 31-34; John 12: 20-33

I will put my law within them, and I will write it on their hearts.
(Jeremiah 31: 33)

I wonder what God meant when God told Jeremiah that the law would be "written on their hearts"?

When I was a boy my father used to tell me that you cannot legislate morality. You can make laws about discrimination, but the laws do not remove prejudice from the human heart. You can make laws about killing, but you will still find murder. You can set speed limits, but people still drive faster than the posted speed.

The old covenant, the Sinai Covenant was written in stone tablets, but the people could not abide by them. That is how Judah and Israel found themselves in exile in foreign lands. We fallen creatures seem to be unable to abide by external laws and rules. Behavior is only changed not externally, but internally; not by the rule of law but a change of heart.

In Jeremiah we read that God was going to imprint, literally carve or tattoo, the law upon the human heart so that it would be a part of who we are. We could act without thinking but out of a sense of habit.

This covenant was to be given not at the time of Jeremiah but in later generations. We, who take Jesus seriously, believe that

He is the new covenant that Jeremiah pointed to. Whereas the first covenant called a people, Jesus called individuals to be a new people, a "peculiar" people. A people what knows what it means to be "saved" or "set apart" to "serve.

In John's gospel Jesus told his disciples that unless a grain of wheat falls to the earth and dies, it remains but a single grain. But if it "loses itself", it's "old self" and "dies" it will bear much fruit. He went on to say that "whoever serves Him must also follow Him and do the work that He does. (John 24-25)

Each week during this season of Lent I have challenged worshipers with a "homework" assignment. This week, if you wish to grow deeper spiritual roots, I encourage you to begin by reflectively reading the New Testament Letter of James, which I believe is "Practically Christianity 101". an intro level course. And then read the Beatitudes in Matthew's gospel. As you read them, ask yourself what God is calling you to do in that letter or that blessing. Pray for the courage and strength to do that which God calls you to do, to live out your insight. Begin your day doing this. And at the end of the day, when you lay down to go to sleep, reflect upon the events of the day and look for those times when God touched you.

To God be the glory. Amen.

How Much Does It Cost?
II Corinthians 8: 7-15

"How much does it cost to join this church?" That question was posed to one of our Executive Board members not too long ago. He was unsure how to answer, so he asked me.

It is not an unreasonable question; after all, don't people say to us, "There is no free lunch"?

We pay to go to the movies, plays, join fraternal and social organizations, and country clubs.

So, how would YOU answer that question?

Some would say that the cost of membership is what is referred to as "the per capita". The per capita is an apportionment that Presbyterians pay to the denomination each year. It is based on a congregation's active members. This year is about $32 per member. We contribute a like amount to the United Church of Christ's Our Church's Wider Mission. I call this a "franchise fee". It covers administrative support from all levels of the greater Church. This summer the Finance Committee had someone from the Presbyterian Foundation talk to the committee about the church's endowment policies. The consultation yielded good information and was free.

But, if every member paid only their per capita and nothing more, the church's operating budget would be $20,000 per year. That is not sustainable. Earlier this year the Bethel Presbyterian

Church on the Southside of Peoria dissolved their congregation and their annual budget was larger than $20,000 a year.

Maybe the cost of membership should be based on the cost of Sunday worship. Each week we invest approximately $2,497.30 in our worship service, not including utilities, insurance and various miscellaneous items. Should a fee be charged at the door? Where's the grace in that!

Maybe membership costs should be figured on a carte blanche basis, that is you pay for only for ministries that you like or use. But then, some less attractive things would go wanting, things like utilities, insurance, repairs and the like.

Maybe a church should be like a country club and have a yearend assessment! But then, it wouldn't be a church, would it? It would be a country club open to only a select few.

There are all kinds of ways to answer the question, "How much does it cost to join the church?"

But maybe, just maybe, "How much does it cost to join the church?" is the wrong question. Have you ever considered that?

If you ask the wrong question you will not get the right answer.

Maybe the price of membership has already been paid! Maybe it was paid 2000 years ago on a hill far away, on a cross.

In his letter to the Corinthians the apostle Paul wrote:

For you know the generous act of our Lord Jesus Christ, that though he was rich, yet for your sakes he became poor, so that by his poverty you might become rich. (II Corinthians 8: 9; my emphasis)

In a later letter the apostle wrote that "we were reconciled to God through the death of his Son. How much more, having been reconciled, shall we be saved through Him?" (Romans 5:10)

The baptismal font and the Lord's Table are visible signs of an invisible truth--that the cost of membership into the Body of Christ, the Church has been paid in full.

If that's the case, then a more appropriate question would be the one that the Old Testament prophet Micah asked nearly a century before Christ: With what shall I come before the Lord, and bow myself before God on high? (6:6)

In other words, how do I respond to God's grace in my life? "Praise God from Whom all blessings flow." "Count your many blessings, one by one," the old hymn says. How much are those blessings worth? What is your ROI--Return on Investment?

In his sermon on the Mount Jesus said "where you treasure is, there will be your heart also. (Matthew 5: 21). A corollary is that how we send our money reveals what we treasure.

Today's epistle lesson does not encourage poverty. It encourages generosity.

As the apostle Paul wrote,

I do not mean; it is a question of balance between your abundance and their need. (v. 13) ... Each of you must give as you have made up your mind, not reluctantly or under compulsion, for God loves a cheerful giver. And God is able to provide you with every blessing in abundance, so that by always having enough, you may share abundantly. (vss. 7,8)

So, "How much does it cost to join the church?"

That's the wrong question. The right question is, "What shall I bring unto the Lord?"

To God be the glory. Amen.

The Power of Words
James 1: 17-27

I any think they are religious, and do not bridle their tongues but deceive their hearts, their religion is worthless. (v. 22)

I fell in love with the Letter of James at a time in my life when I felt overwhelmed by the tasks and responsibilities of life. It was at a time before I went to seminary or was even very active in the life of the church. Seeking guidance and feeling as if I had nowhere else to turn--or maybe thinking that I had nothing to lose--I pulled a Bible off of my small bookshelf and accidently--or Providentially--opened it to the book of James. And there I read,

If any of you lack wisdom, let him ask of God, that giveth to all people liberally, and upbraideth not, and it shall be given. But ask in faith, not waveth. For he that waveth is like a wave of the sea driven with the wind and tossed. For let that that person think that he shall receive any thing of the Lord. A double minded person is unstable in all his ways. (vss. 5&6) In case you haven't guessed it was a King James Bible; the bible I received from my home church years earlier. Nothing fancy. Fake leather with no inscription. We Boomers didn't have helicopter moms and dads and were too numerous to have much personal attention.

My doctoral thesis was on infant baptism and the role of a congregation in the spiritual nurture of a child. It was then that I concluded that our faith is not taught as much as it is caught.

That is why I call the epistle of James "Christianity 101". If someone is wants to know how to have a Christian lifestyle, I tell them to read James.

The earliest Christians did not have doctrine but practice. Acts tells us that they gathered together on the first day of the week to sing hymns, share a meal, have fellowship and one of their number would share a story of Jesus and His teachings. From this humble beginning the Christian faith exploded across the known Western world not because of its teachings but because of its living. Others saw how they loved each other, cared for each other, looked after "the orphans and the widows in their distress" and remained "unstained" by the culture of the world.

In his book, *The Monday Connection,* William E. Diehl wrote:

"In today's world "Sunday Christians" are irrelevant. The hymns, sermons, prayers, and creeds of Sunday morning have no impact upon the outside world unless they share the lives of Christians during the rest of the week. The false idols and pernicious values of society remain unchallenged unless 'Monday Christians' act and witness to their faith in everyday life in a relevant manner. ...

"For the majority of churchgoing people, Sunday morning is the time to get away from the cares of the world and to think about 'spiritual' things. Sunday worship is a refuge from the world. When pressed to explain how the Sunday experience relates to their daily lives, people frequently respond that they gain strength for the rest of the week. when asked how the strength shows up in their daily lives, however, they become vague." (p.1)

Be doers of the word, James wrote, not merely hearers.

Today's lesson challenges those of us who commit to taking Jesus seriously to be living testimonies of the One whom we worship.

It seems to me that the biggest challenges we face in being living testimonies of Christ is our words. Anyone who watched the funeral services of the late Senator John McCain or Aretha Franklin this past weekend knows the power of words to bring move our emotions.

"Words create a world of meaning."

We use words to express ourselves; to convince and convict, to describe, name, blame and label. We use words to win arguments, expound a point, explain things into or out of existence, persuade, condole, console, and counsel. We use words to announce and denounce. We use words to ask someone to marry, to declare war or peace, to sentence someone to punishment, diagnose a condition, analyze a problem, deliberate, debate or negotiate a deal.

"We cannot get along without words. Words can alarm, harm, inspire, degrade or silence" another. Words can express some of our inner thoughts.

According to James, we cannot be partners with God in building the Kingdom on earth through revengeful or evil speech, "which" he says, "only spreads destruction."

Such speech poisons our own lives and the communities of which we are a part. (The last three paragraphs are freely quoted from Archie Smith, Jr., in the commentary *Feasting on the Word, Year B, Volume 4, Season After Pentecost*).

Over the next few weeks we will look more closely at how we can be doers of the word; the Word incarnate in Jesus Christ. This week I invite you to join me in reflecting upon the words we choose to use.

One tool may be The Four-Way Test of what we think, say or do. Written by Herbert J. Taylor it has found its way into service clubs (notably Rotary) and even the courtrooms of Ghana, west Africa. It consists of four simple but profound questions;

Is it true?

Is it fair?

Will it build goodwill?

Is it beneficial to all concerned?

Another tool may be one developed by Celeste Headlee, the host of the NPR program, "On Second Thought". A couple of years ago she did a Ted Talk on 10 Ways to have a better conversation. Here are her ten:

1. Listen. "If your mouth is open, you are not learning.

2. Don't multitask but be present.

3. Don't pontificate. "You have to enter every conversation assuming that you have something to learn … sometimes that means setting aside your personal opinion.

4. Use open ended questions.

5. Go with the flow.

6. If you don't know, say you don't know.

7. Don't equate your experience with their experience.

8. Try not to repeat yourself.

9. Stay out of the weeds. People don't care about the years, names, the dates, that you may struggle with.

10. Be brief.

And with that, To God Be the Glory. Amen.

Can Faith Save You?
James 2: 1-17

> *What good is it, my brothers and sisters, if you say you have faith but do not have works? Can faith save you?* (verse 14)

The writer of James is flabbergasted. You heard the lesson. He seems to be saying, how can you in good conscience give preferential treatment to one person over another? Once comes in with gold rings and fine clothes and you say, "Have a seat here, please. This is one of the best seats in the house!" And another person who is poor is shown to the narthex or the balcony. How can you in good conscience and Christ's name make such distinctions?

Someone once told me that I needed to visit a newcomer in town not because they expressed any interest in the church but because, and I quote, "they are rich". What an odd thing to say to a minister of Word and Sacrament. It made me feel sorry for the rich person. How could she ever be sure that someone liked her, wanted to spend time with her or be her friend? Wouldn't she always wonder if the relationship was built on genuine friendship or was it built on what she could give? I think that this is why many presidents of the United States maintain their closest relationships with those who knew them before they became the most powerful person in the world. They hang on their grade school and high school and college friends because they knew them "when"; when they weren't burdened by the trappings of this world.

In his book, *The Little Prince*, Antoine Saint-Exupéry wrote about "grown-ups" and our "grown up bias".

"Grownups love figures. When you tell them that you have made a new friend, they never ask you any questions about essential matters. They never say to you, 'What does his voice sound like? What games does he love best? Does he collect butterflies?' Instead they demand: 'How old is he? How many brothers has he? How much does he weigh? How much money does his father make?' Only from these figures do they think they have learned anything about him.

"If you were to says to the grown-ups: 'I saw a beautiful house made of rosy brick, with geraniums in the windows and doves on the roof,' they would not be able to get any idea of that housed at all. You would have to tell them how much it cost. Then they would exclaim: 'Oh, what a pretty house that is!'"

The late homiletics profession and preacher once told the story of the story of seeing two beautiful sixteen-year-old girls within the span of a week or two. The first girl word a beautiful blue dress and was coming down a spiral staircase to the applause of an admiring groups of family and friends.

The second girl, a couple of weeks later, was equally pretty. She was standing on the porch of a mountain cabin in Kentucky. She held a young child whose father was long gone. She was standing on the porch alone with a half-dozen scrawny chickens pecking in the yard. She lived in a gray world without much hope.

In his prayers that evening, the late homiletics professor Fred Craddock asked God, "Did you notice the difference? Why is it in this world, does one sixteen-year old walk down a spiral staircase, while another sixteen-year-old stands on the porch of a poor shack with a baby in her arms? Now, why the difference?"

He began to think that maybe God was getting a little old, slipping a bit, if you know what I mean. But as Craddock thought of this possibility a little voice appeared in his head. It was the still small voice of God. It said, "What difference? I don't see a difference."

The apostle Paul wrote in his letter to the Romans that this is no difference between the Greek and Jews for it is the same Lord who is Lord of all. (Romans 10:12)

And in the letter to the Galatians Paul wrote" In Christ's family there can be no difference between Jew and non-Jew, slave and free, male and female. Among us you are all equal. That is, we are all in a common relationship with Jesus Christ. Also, since you are Christ's family, then you are Abraham's famous 'descendant,' heirs according to the covenant promises.

Visible reminders of this invisible and eternal truth sit in our chancel area each time we worship; the baptismal font and behind it the communion table. We are baptized not because who we are but because of Whose we are--God's precious children created in the Divine image. And we dare share the bread and fruit of the vine from the table not because we are worthy but because we are part of God's eternal family, adopted children of the Creator of the ends of the earth.

So, on to the question of day; "Can faith save you?" Jesus once said that you can tell the nature of a tree by the fruit that it produces. We betray what we believe in, we betray our true faith by the decisions we make and lives that we live. When in the name of our so-called "faith" when we draw distinctions between ourselves and others, divide the world into "us" and "them", those who agree with us and those who disagree, those who are rich and those who are poor, those whose skin color is a different shade from ours, or whose languages and customs are not the same as ours, and those who vote differently than we do.

But it is real and alive when despite these surface differences we can see the face of God in the face of the other, for they have been saved by the same amazing grace by which we ourselves are saved by.

To God be the glory. Amen.

Tongues of Fire

James 3: 1-12

"And the tongue is a fire..." (v 6)

I was privileged to officiate at a wedding last night. The party favor for the guests at the reception was the fixings for s'mores with the largest marshmallow that I have ever seen! This is the perfect time of year for evening fires, roasting marshmallows and having fellowship in the cool night air. Those of us of a certain age may remember church camp fires when someone would pull out a guitar and we'd sing. "It only takes a spark to get a fire going, and soon all those around can warm up in its glowing".

Fire. It can create memories, and it can just as easily destroy.

One of my warm memories is of a visit that I had with an elderly woman named Olive Stewart. Olive lived on a very rustic farm near Princeville. Driving down the long narrow lane and coming upon the tiny house that had been built a half century ago, a house that, at one time, she shared with her brother Carl. Getting out of the car you had to dodge banty chickens that swarmed around your legs. Walking through the low wooden gate you saw a neat little yard and a porch surrounded by spring and summer flowers.

My father lived with the Stewarts the summer after his mother died unexpectedly. He was 15 years old and his whole world had fallen apart. He used to tell stories of helping Carl in the field, pitching square bales on the back of a hay wagon.

I remember one visit with Olive very specifically. It was before I was married. I spent the morning doing some odd jobs around her place when she insisted that I enjoy a hot lunch. I watched her prepare a very simply meal in an old stove that she fueled with corn cobs. The glow of the fire in the stove fed the fellowship and physical nourishment that I shared with Olive that day. It's funny, but I hadn't thought of that in over 40 years.

It's kind of like the fire of Pentecost; the Holy Spirit descending upon the gathered disciples empowering them to spread the word of God's saving love and grace witnessed to in the life, death and, most importantly, resurrection of Jesus Christ.

Yet, fire can also destroy, can't it. As of the end of July over 13,000 firefighters battled 12 large wildfires in California. These fires burned over 688,000 acres or 1000 square miles, destroying homes and other structures.

When we started this series on the Letter of James, I said that it is Christianity 101. It tells us how we live out our baptism and live together in community as a witness to the One Whom we call Lord.

How we speak to our about one another is a barometer of our health as a community of faith.

Do we build up or tear down?

Do we gossip or speak truth in love?

Do we seek reconciliation or sow the seeds of division?

Our words, as well as our actions are the true witness to the world outside of the faith community. Gandhi is reported to have said that he was a great admirer of Jesus and that he would readily become a Christian if he ever met one!

Adam Hamilton, the senior minister of the Resurrection United Methodist Church in Kansas City, once told the story of riding the car of one of his best friends. The friend had decided to place a church bumper sticker on his car that read, "I follow Jesus".

Well, as fate would have it, as they rode along someone pulled in front of Hamilton and his friend just before a stop light. The friend hit the break, honked and probably muttered a few things perhaps adding a hand gesture. Sometime things escalate. When the light turned green Hamilton's friend zipped around the offender, pulled in front of him and slowed way down. The driver, now behind them, honked his horn. At the next stop light both drivers jumped out of their cars. It was at this time that Adam Hamilton heard the driver behind him shout, "Is that what following Jesus looks like?!"

He goes on to say, "Don't put something on your bumper you're not willing to try to live".

The lesson, though, is also true of social media. "It's so easy to express our feelings using social media without the filters we would use if we were speaking to someone face to face. We post snarky comments about another, or to another.

We hurl 280-character zingers at one another. The Tweet limit used to be 140 characters, but it seems that we now have so much more to say!

And we often pass on gossip, innuendo and outright lies about other people as we forward things, we assume are true, without finding out if they really are. The Bible calls this, literally, gossip and backbiting.

I remember being with a youth group once when a member of the group said something nasty about someone else. One of his peers asked, "Do you kiss your mama with that mouth?"

From the same mouth come blessing and cursing, James writes, my brothers and sisters, this ought not be so. Does a spring pour forth from the same opening both fresh and brackish water? (v. 10)

There's a story that I am sure is apocryphal but true in the truest sense of the word. A grandfather is speaking to his grandchild. "A fight is going on inside me," he said to the boy."

It is a terrible fight and it is between two wolves. One is evil–he is anger, envy, sorrow, regret, greed, arrogance, self-pity, guilt, resentment, inferiority, lies, false pride, superiority, and ego."

He continued, "The other is good – he is joy, peace, love, hope, serenity, humility, kindness, benevolence, empathy, generosity, truth, compassion, and faith. The same fight is going on inside you–and inside every other person, too."

The grandson thought about it for a minute and then asked his grandfather: "Which wolf will win?"

The grandfather replied, "The one you feed."

"It only takes a spark to get a fire going, and soon all those around can warm up in its glowing; that's how it is with God's love, once you've experienced it: you spread God's love to everyone, you want to pass it on."

Each week in this sermon series I have given you a homework assignment. This week's assignment is to think before you speak, tweet, post, or forward. Ask yourself if it builds or destroys, sews together or rends apart. Ask if it is God glorifying or denigrating to someone created in the very image of God. Amen.

Grace Along the Appalachian Trail
John 10: 11-18

Since 1980 I have been part of a weekly clergy study group that explores and shares ideas about sermon texts. Since pastor Zach has been on our staff, we've included something called lectio divina. This is a form of prayer study in which one person reads the text aloud, and we reflect upon what jumps out to us. This passage in John's gospel has always been a favorite of mine because of a particular verse, "I have other sheep that do not belong to this fold...and they will listen to my voice". (v. 16) But this last week, another verse or phrase also jumped out at me. "I lay (my life) down of my own accord. I have power to lay it down, and I have power to take it up again." (v. 18) I am going to share with you the insights that came to me as I studied this passage.

First, would you join me in prayer? Lord God may the words of my mouth and the meditations of our hearts be acceptable to you. May everything said that is true be engraved on every heart and anything said that is false be quickly forgotten and cause no harm. Amen.

I have other sheep not of this fold. Jesus was speaking to his disciples, to those he called and those who seriously followed him. In this text he told them that there are people outside of their little group--sheep that do not belong to "this fold". They, too, know the Master's voice. In his commentary on John, John Calvin noted that there are, in reality, two churches: The Visible and the Invisible. The Visible Church is the church that gathers on Sunday mornings. The Invisible Church, the True Church, is the Church known only to God. It is possible, he went on to say, that not everyone in the Visible Church is a member of the Invisible Church, and it is definitely true that not everyone in the Invisible Church is a part of the Visible Church.

Faithfulness is known by the fruit it produces. Good trees, Jesus said, cannot produce bad fruit and bad trees cannot produce good fruit. The Apostle Paul picked up on this theme when he wrote that the "fruit of the spirit" is Love, Joy, Peace, Patience, Kindness, Goodness, Faithfulness, Humility, and Self-control while the fruits of the world cause nothing but divisions, jealousy, mistrust, and ultimately destruction.

In the synoptic gospels of Matthew, Mark and Luke, Jesus called his disciples to be "fishers of men." He did not call then to be "keepers of the aquarium". Those who take him seriously are to go out onto the wild waters of life and, to mix metaphors, find the sheep not of the visible fold. We are to be a light in darkness, an alarm clock that awakens people to the salvation that is already theirs. We are called to show the broken a new Way of life, one that reveals real truth and real life.

I lay (my life) down of my own accord. I have power to lay it down, and I have power to take it up again." This is John's equivalent of picking up Christ's Cross. You know there is a difference between a Cross and a Thorn in the Side. We have a choice when it comes to the Cross of Christ. We do not have a choice when it comes to a Thorn in the Side. My stutter may be seen as a Thorn--it is just a given, a part of who I am. A Cross, though, is something that we choose; we choose to take Jesus seriously. We choose to embrace his teachings and apply them to our lives.

If you walk the Appalachian Trail where hikers cross from Pennsylvania into New Jersey, you will see The Presbyterian Church of the Mountain, a small country church seemingly in the middle of nowhere. Walking up its steep gravel driveway between March and November, you will see a grassy knoll with an array of colorful pitched pup tents. Near the tents you will see plastic lawn chairs doubling as drying racks draped with underwear, trousers, shorts and soggy socks, open backpacks, and worn hiking boots getting dried out and a good airing. If you go inside the church you will see that the basement has been transformed into a hostel, of sorts, complete with a communal living, restrooms, a bunk room and showers. During the peak season this oasis serves a hot dinner, fresh towels and transportation for those who need a doctor or emergency or even a few supplies at nearby stores.

Through this ministry to the hikers of the Appalachian Trail a once dying church experienced a resurrection. In 1976 they had 15 worshipers. Facing death they experienced Resurrection. They could have done one of two things; they could have circled the wagons and looked inward or throw caution to the wind and take "a flyer". The chose the latter course. They chose, in the words of Jesus, to willing lay their lives down for God's sheep that lay outside of their fold. They knew that God has planted them there and sustained them through the years to be a blessing and an outpost to the world and their community. They asked themselves how they could live out their "call", their baptism. How could they show God's love to the world? Through discussion and prayer--and resistance and more prayer--they ultimately decided to open their church building to the Appalachian Trail hikers whom they had never met. It was a risky proposition, but they took their discipleship seriously.

Today, the church is no longer on the brink of extinction. They are thriving. They found new life through this ministry of hospitality. Over the years they have ministered to Austria, Germany, Australia, Scotland and nearly every state in the Union.

In her book, *A Course in Miracles,* Marianne Williamson wrote:

"Our deepest fear is not that we are inadequate. Our deepest fear is that we are powerful beyond measure. It is our light, not our darkness that most frightens us. We ask ourselves, 'Who am I to be brilliant, gorgeous, talented, fabulous?' Actually, who are you not to be? You are a child of God. You're playing small does not serve the world. There is nothing enlightened about shrinking so that other people won't feel insecure around you. We are all meant to shine, as children do. We were born to make manifest the glory of God that is within us. It's not just in some of us; it's in everyone. And as we let our own light shine, we unconsciously give other people permission to do the same. As we are liberated from our own fear, our presence automatically liberates others."

The Kingdom of God is like a mustard seed, Jesus once said. It may be "small", but it does not remain small. It grows. The Presbyterian Church of the Mountain knew that doing the same thing and expecting different results was the very definition of insanity. Rather than play small, they decided to take Jesus seriously--take the risk of discipleship reaching out to their neighbors and the world around them. In our gospel lesson Jesus talked about willingly laying his life down.

Over the past ten years, I have volunteered an hour a week at a local elementary school reading to and being read to by second graders. Not too long ago I was troubled when one of my young students told me, before we started reading, that she had not had breakfast yet. She was late getting to school. Now you may not be aware of the fact that every child in our citywide school district gets a free breakfast to start their day. I knew that my little charge would not be able to focus with an empty growling stomach, so I took her to the cafeteria. The breakfast crew was still there. Their stations were still set up. There was a milk station, a food station, a fruit station and a juice station. I was troubled when I learned that at the milk station my student has to choose between a piece of string cheese and a carton of milk. She could not have both. Her milk choice was white or chocolate. Well, you know what she chose; chocolate milk. At the food station she was given a frosted pop tart. At the fruit station an apple. At the juice station, a carton of sweetened apple juice. So, she walked away with all of the elements of a "sugar high"; chocolate mill, frosted pop tart, an apple that she may or may not eat, and apple juice.

I talked to head of nutrition and was told that the government program that makes breakfast possible only allows one milk product. I think that it could be argued that chocolate milk is on the edge of the milk food group compared to a piece of string cheese or white milk. I got to thinking, it these children are dependent upon a school breakfast, what do they do during the summer when school is no longer in session.

This church has done an excellent job in the area of mission. The flags in the back of the sanctuary remind us of all the countries that we have done mission. The most recent flag--that of Kenya--reminds us of the street boys of Mombasa, Kenya who have a new start because we planted a group home and continue to support that ministry called Wana Wa Mola--Swahili for "God's Children". This year we will build our sixth Habitat house, the second most houses built by a congregation. Every week volunteers gather in the Life Together Center and pack over 200 weekend snack packs for the children of Whittier elementary school and Common Place. As I reflected upon all of this, I wondered why it wouldn't be possible for us to help feed a healthy breakfast to the students of Thomas Jefferson during the summer months. We have the talent pool and the resources for this ministry. I would like for us to pray and explore whether or not this is a ministry that God is calling us to do.

We have been richly blessed. We have been saved to serve. It does no one any favors to "play small". We do not serve a small God, but a God that is bigger than the Universe and Eternity itself.

To God be the glory. Amen.

God in the Silence
Luke 2: 41-52

And Jesus increased in wisdom and in years (strength), and in divine and human favor. (v. 52)

Today's lesson is the only story that we have of Jesus' boyhood. But even in this story, we know very little about his early years for the story of a twelve-year-old Jesus finds him on the cusp of adulthood. We know very little about his early years. Some people call this period in his life "the silent years". The gospel of Mark is completely silent on the matter. His gospel begins with the call of John the Baptist and Jesus baptism. John's gospel is equally silent. His gospel echoes the Creation story the begins the Old Testament book of "beginnings"; Genesis. "In the beginning was the Word, and the Word was with God, and the Word was God. ... All things were made by him; and without him was not anything made that was made. (1: 1, 3 KJV) According to John, then, Jesus is God, the One who was at the Beginning and whose Word brought everything into existence.

Matthew speaks only of Jesus birth, the wise men, the family's flight into Egypt, and the killing of the innocent. Luke gives us the main elements of what we think of as "the Christmas story"; the annunciation by the angel Gabriel, the birth of Jesus, the announcing angel and accompanying heavenly hosts, the shepherds in the field at night, and his dedication in the Temple--Simeon's blessing and the prophetic words of Anna.

By and large we don't think very much about Jesus boyhood. But there is no reason to think that if Jesus is fully human and fully divine, the very incarnation of God, the visible manifestation of the invisible God, as the letter to the Colossians says, was not like other boys. He was fed and bathed and tucked into bed at night; played in the streets of Nazareth, had a best friend or two, even got into a little mischief from time to time. I suppose that he probably had a favorite food and had some foods that he was not terribly fond of eating. I imagine that he even followed his dad around, as little boys often do. Since Joseph is not mentioned as being present in Jesus later life, I suppose that Jesus grieved at Joseph's grave. But other than these events, there is silence.

Silence makes us uncomfortable. Listen to the coughs during an extended silent prayer or notice the nervous shifting of us. How long can we drive without turning on the radio because we cannot stand the silence? It's almost as if any noise is better than no We are startled by silence in this world of continue background noise and mood music. Silence forces us to come face to face with ourselves. There are no shiny objects, no squirrels, no distractions.

Richard J. Foster speaks of a "purifying silence" of the soul. This silence is not dramatic. Rather, it is subtle, gradual not unlike the realization that a child has grown by noticing the pencil marks on a hallway door jam. (Prayer: Finding the Heart's True Home, p. 21)

The early Christian mystic St. John of the Cross referred to the silence of God as "the dark night of the soul". This silence strips us of two things. First it strips us of our dependence on exterior "things". "We find ourselves less and less impressed with the religion of the 'big deal'--big buildings, big budgets, big productions, big miracles. Not that there is anything wrong with big things, but they (just) no longer impress us.

The second stripping is of our dependence upon exterior "results." In this stripping we become more aware of how little in life we really control. In this stripping we grasp how little control we have for our own destiny. We are at the mercy of others more than we like to think or admit. (ibid. p. 22)

God is often found in the silence.

The Old Testament the prophet Elijah sought the voice of the Lord in the strong wind, the fire, and the earthquake, but the Lord's voice was not found in any of the three. The voice of the Lord was found in a still small voice. And it was a voice of courage, and determination, and promise.

God works in silence.

George McDonald once wrote that when God wants an important thing done in this world or a wrong righted, God goes about it in a very singular way. God's doesn't release thunderbolts or stir up earthquakes. God simply has a tiny baby born, perhaps of very humble parents. God puts an idea in the parent's heart, and they, in turn put it in the child's mind. And then, God waits.

The great events of this world are not battles or elections or earthquakes or even thunderbolts. The world's great events are babies, for each child comes with the message that God is not yet discouraged with us--with humanity. God is still expecting that goodwill will become incarnate in each and every human life. (Paraphrased)

In silence God makes every moment our ordinary lives holy. It was in the devotions of Brother Lawrence that I first realized God sanctifies even the washing of dishes and taking out the garbage, going to work and working on calculous. There are no real ordinary times or wasted moments under God's watchful eye. Every moment counts. The Psalmist reminds us that God is "acquainted with all our ways--our sitting down and rising up; even our thoughts from afar." (Psalm 139) Understanding this can't help but to give us pause in this hurry up, quick-fix, instant-oatmeal, smartphone world.

In the silent years of Jesus faith matured. He developed the habit of worship. Our gospel lesson reminds us that Jesus' parents had "a custom" of going to the Temple in Jerusalem every year during Passover. And later in Luke's gospel we are told that Jesus had the habit of worship. It was this habit that took him to his hometown of Nazareth where he was handed the scroll Isaiah to read during worship.

The Spirit of the Lord is upon me, he read, "because He has anointed me to preach good news to the poor; ... proclaim release to the captives ... sight to the blind ... liberty to the oppressed, and to proclaim the acceptable year of the Lord (Luke 4: 18-19)

He then closed the scroll and declared that this word has been fulfilled in their hearing.

In the silence of the Temple Jesus told his parents that he "must be about his Father's business." If we, as a Christian community, are the body of Christ in this time and this place then we, too, must be about the Father's business. We are called to embody compassion, kindness, humility, gentleness, patience, forgiveness, love, peace, and thanksgiving.

Quite frankly, though, these qualities are increasingly hard to find in today's culture. They are said to be naive; they may be ok for the weak or the naive or the "baby Jesus, meek and mild" but they are not "real world" stuff, not in this world of villainizing those with whom we disagree.

Those who decide to take Jesus seriously do not measure themselves by the standards of the world, though. We know that there is a higher standard, a higher calling, a higher measure. The letter to the Colossians invites us to be wise, mature people understanding that there is a greater Reality than this time limited on in which we live and move and have our being. We are invited to live into our baptism vows and nourished at the Lord's Table. In the words of the apostle, "God's chosen ones, holy and beloved" (3:12), be a Light to the nations. Bring a word of Hope to the world. Do this to the glory of God. Amen.

Amen.

Under Armour
Ephesians 6

> *Our struggle is not against enemies of blood and flesh, but against the rulers, against the authorities, against the cosmic powers of this present darkness, against the spiritual forces of evil in the heavenly place.* (v.12)

This is my grandfather Jaynes' cane. He said that he needed it in order to keep dogs away when he went on his daily walks, but I suspect that it was to help keep him be steady on his feet.

Several years ago in Venice, Florida the mother of a martial arts instructor named Buck Buckmaster was attacked coming out of a grocery store. She was knocked to the ground and robbed. In response to this incident Buckmaster decided to offer a self-defense course to the residents of the retirement community where his mother lived. Using their canes, walkers, purses and whatever else they may have the residents learn how to defend themselves from attacks. Attackers do not want a fight. They do not want to risk injury. They want to hit and run so an aggressive defense will dissuade most attackers.

There is a YouTube video showing the residents going through their self-defense exercises. In an interview the residents talked about how they felt empowered. They didn't feel vulnerable. They knew what to do. They had an air of unmistakable confidence.

In our epistle lesson today the writer concluded this letter by talking about battling the great forces of evil in this world.

Robert Louis Stevenson once wrote,

"You know the Caledonian Railway in Edinburgh? One cold east windy morning I met Satan there."

We do not know what happened at that Edinburgh Railway, but I believe that we all know what Stevenson meant. We have all experienced the icy touch of evil that chills the bones and sends a shiver down the spine.

The personification of evil is not central to the biblical understanding of evil. That is not to say that evil is not personal. People are not evil, but people do evil things. Evil is a force that hypnotizes people and nations. It is like a nebulous cloud blanketing and infecting those whom it envelopes. Evil appeals to our lesser angels.

It is the Tempter in the Garden who told Eve that if she ate the forbidden fruit, she would not die but become wise like God. Evil plays to our fears and insecurities telling us that we are weak, vulnerable and "not such a much". It sows gossip. That is why gossip is one of the sins that the New Testament epistles focus so much attention upon. Evil feeds red meat to our prejudices-- after all, you may remember that one has to be very carefully taught.

In the musical, *South Pacific*, one of the songs says,

You've got to be taught
To hate and fear,
You've got to be taught
From year to year,
It's got to be drummed
In your dear little ear
You've got to be carefully taught.
You've got to be taught to be afraid
Of people whose eyes are oddly made,
And people whose skin is a diff'rent shade,
You've got to be carefully taught.
You've got to be taught before it's too late,
Before you are six or seven or eight,
To hate all the people your relatives hate,
You've got to be carefully taught!

*****

Evil is the green eyes of jealousy and the heat of hatred.

Evil gives rise to feelings of privilege, systematic discrimination and self-justification. Evil dehumanizes and objectifies. It causes crushing poverty, stupid famine, war, and senseless mindless shootings in our cities.

These enemies are not mere flesh and blood. No, they are the cosmic powers of darkness. They are the spiritual forces of evil in heavenly places.

In the face of evil, we are to be dressed for battle. We are to put on the defensive armor of Truth, Righteousness and Proclaim the gospel of Peace.

We are to lift the shield of Faith--Faith is the assurance of things hoped for and the conviction of things unseen. (Hebrews 11:1)

Most of all, we are constant in prayer. We are to pray to be alert. We are to pray for each other. We are to pray and stand by the persecuted, the misunderstood, the marginalized and the forgotten.

And do you know why we do this? We do this because we are baptized ambassadors of God's kingdom heralds of that Kingdom here on earth who defiantly and boldly proclaim the gospel of the One who is the Light of the World. We do it for the glory of God that the glory of God alone.

Be Careful How You Live
Ephesians 5: 15-20

Be careful how you lived, not as unwise people but as wise, making the most of the time because the days are evil. (v. 1)

The clock of life is wound but once,
and no (one) has the power,
to tell just when that clock will stop.
at late or early hour.
Now is the only time you own,
live...love...toil with the will.
Place no faith into tomorrow, for the clock may then be still.

*****

On a wall there hangs a counted cross stitch that my wife made for her father. It reads:

Do you love life?
Then do not waste time
For that is what life is made of.

The late Dr. Wayne Oates, Professor of Psychiatry and Behavioral Sciences at the University of Louisville once told the story in his book, *Your Right to Rest*, of a professor that he had at Wake Forest University in North Carolina.

"Wayne," the professor would say, "I want you to tell me in two or three sentences what you are doing today to justify the good Lord's wisdom when he gives you the air to breathe!" And in the laughter of good friends, Dr. Oates would try to answer the question. (Your Right to Rest, Westminster Press, c. 1984, p. 40)

I have a question for you to consider. What is the fulcrum of your life?

"Be careful how you live..." the writer of Ephesians advised.

Make wise decisions.

In Ephesians the fulcrum is found in the gathered worshiping community.

It is found when the people of God gather together to sing psalms and hymns, pray together, support one another, have fellowship with one another and hear the Living Word of God proclaimed in all of its comforting, challenging and troubling dimensions.

True worship is not found in one style or another whether it be contemporary or traditional or blended, Pentecostal with "happy hands" lifted high or folded hands and bowed heads.

It is not found in stale tradition, rote prayers and statements or manipulated passions. Rather, it is found in a community bound together--knit together--by the Holy Spirit committed to living out the heart of the faith; one Lord, one faith, one baptism; one God and Father of all, who is over all and through all and in all. (Ephesians 4: 4-6)

There is a South African word, ubuntu, which captures this sense of being bound together under God. Archbishop Desmond Tutu defined ubuntu in these words.

It is to say, "My humanity is caught up, is inextricably bound up in yours." We belong in a bundle of life. We say, "A person is a person through other persons." It is not "I think, therefore I am". It is rather, "I am human because I belong. I participate. I share." (Such a person) is open and available to others, affirming of others ... (because they have) a proper self-assurance that comes from knowing that that he or she belongs in a greater whole and is diminished when others are humiliated or diminished, ... or treated as if they were less than they are."

*****

For as long as there has been humanity there has been an innate impulse to worship. Worship is not about getting our batteries charged for another week--though that may happen. Nor is it about feeling good about ourselves--though that may happen.

It is about praising the God from Whom all blessings flow.

Worship redeems time by drawing our gaze from ourselves and lift it heavenward toward God.

True worship is the outpouring of a heart filled with gratitude.

The spirit of gratitude does not deny the existence of evil. Worship does not ignore the dark corners of this world; persecution, famine, war, disease, abuse, neglect, prejudice, discrimination, privilege.

Gratitude refuses, though, to limit God's Presence, God's Sovereignty.

In the book, *The Dark Night of the Soul,* Gerald May wrote:

"I must confess I am no longer good at telling the difference between good things and bad things. Of course, there are many events in human history that can only be labeled as evil, but from the standpoint of inner individual experience the distinction has become blurred for me. Some things start out looking great but wind up terribly, while other things seem bad in the beginning but turn out to be blessings in disguise ...

"I (believe) that the dark night of the soul reveals a deeper divine activity: a continually gracious, loving, and fundamentally protective guidance through all human experience--the good as well as the bad."

The important thing is not whether we think that an event is good or bad. What matters is discovering God's Presence in every circumstance of life.

The days may be evil, but our lives are not evil, and the One who gives life is not evil but good. The attitude of thanksgiving and a discipline of giving thanks in worship orients our lives toward God. It is only by living all of life to the glory of God that we live into eternity.

To God be the glory.

It's Not About You

Ephesians 2: 1-10

Have your ever wondered if you're "good enough"? Good enough to go to heaven? Have you ever woken up in the early morning hours and wondering? If so, maybe you can take comfort in knowing that the Protestant Reformer Martin Luther had the same worry. As a German monk he prayed to St. Anne to make him "righteous enough". He fasted and confessed and did penitence and practiced all of the spiritual disciplines of the Church, but he could never get the feeling that he was "good enough" or that he had "done enough". And then one night as he read Romans 1: 17 Paul's words jumped out at him, "We are made righteous through faith". Being good enough, being righteous enough, is not about what we do; it is about faith. And Faith is a gift from God.

In today's lesson we read, for by faith you have been saved through faith, and this is not your own doing; it is the gift of God--not the result of works, lest anyone should boast. (vss. 8&9)

Did you hear that? Really hear it? Faith is a gift not a work. You don't have to earn enough points to hit the magic "heavenly score." As a matter of fact, even if you did, you couldn't ever do it no matter how hard your tried. Why? Because "all have sinned and fall short of the glory of God." Nor can you go to a spiritual gymnasium and lift "faith weights" because such a gym does not exist.

Faith is like manna. When God provided manna to the Israelites during their 40-year wilderness journey, they were told that they could not save it for a rainy day. God would provide and they would have to learn to trust in God's Promise, God's covenant, to provide their "daily bread." When Corrie ten Boom was a young girl, she frequently worried about whether or not she would have enough faith to die as a martyr for Jesus. This was her worry as her native Holland and much of Europe fell under the boot of Nazi Germany. One night her father spoke to her about this worry as he tucked her into bed. Kneeling beside her bed he asked her, "When you are going to visit family when do I give you your train ticket? A week before? A day before your journey?" "No". she replied, "you give it to me as I get on the train." "That's how it is with Faith," her father continued. "God gives you the faith you need when you need it and not a moment before." That night stuck with her as she and her family entered a concentration camp. It stayed with her as she held her dying sister. It carried her throughout life after the camp.

Last week while I was driving back to Peoria on Route 29, I saw a billboard that simply said, "He first loved us". It had been paid for by the Peoria Rescue Mission. That billboard says it all. When I teach confirmation classes I tell them we are not good to earn "brownie points" or get "stars in the crown". Nor do are we trying to earn our way into "heaven" or "win" "God's love". The baptismal font in the middle of the chancel reminds us of the truth contained in I John 4, namely, "we love God because God first loved us." We do not baptize the worthy or the loveable but the loved. And the communion table that sits directly behind the font reminds us of God continual love that feeds, nurtures and supports us through all of life. The table is not for the worthy but the loved. Our salvation is a done deal. It was signed, sealed and delivered 2000 years ago "on a hill far away". It is not about us but about God.

The reason that we do good works and the lives that we live are our thank you notes to God for what God has done for us in Jesus Christ. Our lives--the decisions that we make, the things that we do and do not do--are not for our edification but God's glorification. God created us in Christ Jesus, the writer of Ephesians said, so that we can do the good works that God prepared for us to do before we were even born.

Between now and Easter Sunday, let us dedicate ourselves to doing all the good that we can, not so that we may win awards or receive honor or even to be remembered but so that God can be glorified. Amen.

www.ingramcontent.com/pod-product-compliance
Lightning Source LLC
Chambersburg PA
CBHW052150110526
44591CB00012B/1928